Jerusalem

JERUSALEM

And Other Jewish Writings
BY MOSES MENDELSSOHN

Translated and Edited
by Alfred Jospe

SCHOCKEN BOOKS • NEW YORK

To My Children

CONTENTS

vii

Jerusalem

INTRODUCTION

Moses Mendelssohn (1729–1786) was a key figure in the struggle for the social and intellectual emancipation of the Jews in Central Europe. His significance lies in the perception and boldness with which he set out to bridge the gap between the ghetto and Europe and pave the way toward the achievement of civic and cultural equality for the Jewish people.[1]

Mendelssohn was a man of unusual versatility. The first Jewish writer to write in German, he was a gifted stylist and literary critic and became a close friend of Lessing's, whose portrait of the Jew in *Nathan the Wise* he inspired. A shy and even a timid person, he fought courageously in the forefront of numerous controversies to win respect and recognition for Jews and Judaism. Though not breaking new paths as a philosopher, he became one of the fashionable thinkers of his time. A philosophical treatise, *Phädon*, modeled after Plato's *Phaedo*, in which he defended the immortality of the soul, brought him fame throughout Europe. Though no profound religious thinker, he became the first to recognize and define the crucial question which has confronted the Jew since the Emancipation: How is one to reconcile the particular Jewish tradition with contemporary culture, the supernaturalism of an ancient faith with the claims of reason and modern science?

1

He attempted to answer these questions in his major philosophical work of Jewish interest, *Jerusalem*.[2] In its first part, he examined the relationship between church and state and outlined an ideal society, and in its second, he defined the nature of religion and set forth his concept of Judaism. His approach reflected the peculiar dualism of his background and orientation. Mendelssohn was a citizen of two worlds—of the ghetto, with its milieu of Jewish learning and loyalties, and of eighteenth-century Enlightenment, with its glorification of man's reason as the supreme judge and arbiter of all human affairs. As a member of the pre-emancipatory Jewish community he continued to hold firmly to the belief in a God who, as the Creator of the world and Giver of all law, had disclosed His will at a particular point in time and space—Sinai—and to a particular people—Israel. In the value structure of this people, every aspect of life—dietary laws, the patterns of family life, legal procedures, educational objectives, individual conduct, and community organization—received its authentication from the conviction that it was derived from Sinai and that the individual was a member of a holy people set apart by God for a divine mission in the drama of cosmic redemption.

But Mendelssohn also inhabited the world of the general literature and philosophy of his time, whose dominant spirit was probably best defined by Immanuel Kant when he admonished his contemporaries, *sapere aude*, "Dare to use your reason." Reason, not supernatural revelation, is the medium through which man can discern what he needs to know in order to attain happiness and fulfillment in this world and gain immortality in the next.

Two conclusions are drawn from this premise. First, since all men are endowed with the capacity to reason, reason is not, and cannot be, the exclusive possession of any individual or group. Consequently, all who use and live by the truths that reason discloses can achieve salvation. Second, divine revelation is logically no longer needed as a source of truth, for, as Locke sees it, revelation cannot disclose any new ideas that cannot be discovered through reflection and the use of reason (though, for Locke, revelation can disclose the *same* truths that we can discover by reason). Both conclusions are utilized by Mendelssohn.

Jerusalem is Mendelssohn's attempt to reconcile philosophically what he was able to fuse in his personal life—unquestioning loyalty to the God of Sinai and the philosophical rationalism of his age. Mendelssohn holds with Locke, Shaftesbury, and Leibniz that there are eternal truths (defined by Leibniz as *vérités de raison*, as distinguished from *vérités de fait*, historical or temporal truths requiring the evidence of sense experience) which are self-evident to reason and can be verified by the canons of logic. Among these truths are the existence and providence of God and the immortality of the soul. Since these truths are self-evident to reason, they do not require disclosure or verification by an act of God's self-revelation.

In adopting this philosophical position, Mendelssohn divorced himself sharply from the approach of earlier Jewish thinkers, especially that of Moses Maimonides (1135–1204), whose works had stimulated Mendelssohn's initial interest in Jewish philosophy.

For Maimonides, our knowledge of truth is derived from two sources, reason and revelation. Revelation is superfluous for the prophet (as he defines the prophet) and the true philosopher, who are able to discover truth by their own reasoning, but it is needed for the masses of the common people who do not know philosophy and are unable to discover the truth by their own efforts. Consequently, it must be communicated to them through revelation. Reason and revelation are the twin sources of the same truth.

Mendelssohn rejected the claim that truth can be derived from two sources. He felt it is superfluous and, therefore, illogical to assume that revelation is needed to disclose a truth at which man can arrive by virtue of his capacity to reason. The ultimate religious verities cannot be communicated to man by revelation, for no revelation or miracle can possibly convince man of the validity of anything his reason cannot understand.

In extending these notions to Judaism, Mendelssohn confronted the fact that Judaism, according to its classic self-image, is based on the covenant between Israel and God, who has revealed His will to the people at Sinai. Yet, if Judaism, according to Mendelssohn, is revealed, it cannot be a religion. And if it is a religion, it cannot have been revealed.

Mendelssohn did not shy away from following his own logic to its conclusion. Judaism cannot be a revealed religion as Jewish tradition claims. Yet for Mendelssohn it is a religion, and in fact the ideal religion, precisely because its basic principles—the affirmation of God's existence and providence—are in complete harmony with the demands of reason. Unlike Christianity, Judaism has no dogmas contrary to reason, no doctrines the faithful have to affirm in order to attain salvation, no mysteries the believer must accept on faith though they may defy understanding.

At the same time, however, Mendelssohn was unable to surrender his faith in the God who spoke at Sinai and whose revelation was, for him, a *vérité de fait*, a historical fact witnessed by the people of Israel with incontrovertible clarity. If the discovery of eternal verities does not require an act of revelation, how could Mendelssohn justify the historicity and content of the revelation at Sinai?

It is at this point that Mendelssohn introduced his famous notion that Judaism is not "revealed religion" but "revealed law." Judaism is not concerned with a man's beliefs but with his actions. It possesses no binding articles of faith choking independent thought. It addresses itself to man's will. It seeks to guide his daily actions but not to control his thoughts. The distinction between "religion" and "law" is crucial to the understanding of Mendelssohn's philosophy. Judaism is not a religion in the strict sense of the word at all, for its religious tenets are not specifically Jewish notions but identical with the principles of the universal religion of reason. What distinguishes the Jew from the non-Jew is not his religion—those teachings which are the common property of all men of reason—but the unique "laws" and commandments revealed at Sinai. These are valid for the Jewish people alone, and their purpose was and is to distinguish the Jew from the non-Jew, to guide his moral and spiritual conduct, to teach him the acts that are conducive to human happiness, to stimulate his imagination, and to make him ponder man's nature and destiny in God's world.

Although Mendelssohn hoped to demonstrate the enduring validity and truth of Judaism by defining it as revealed "law" rather than as revealed "religion," he did not realize that he was merely subtracting from reason what he was granting to revelation. The thinker for whom no belief is valid if it is contrary to reason is compelled by his own logic to declare that all concepts and ideas which are rational by his definition are not Judaism, while Judaism consists solely of those elements which are nonrational, which reason can neither prove nor understand, which have to be accepted on faith, and which God therefore had to disclose to the Jewish people in a trans-rational act of revelation.

Mendelssohn was not aware of the paradox of his position. He saw no contradictions. The God of reason and the God of Sinai are one and the same. For him, God is the benevolent Creator and Sustainer of the world whom his reason can affirm, as well as the King and Guardian of Israel who had ordained the laws governing Jewish life. His personal faith succeeded in harmonizing two worlds which remained philosophically unreconciled: Mendelssohn proclaimed the heteronomous character of Judaism by defining it as revealed law while at the same time asserting its autonomous character by defining religion as a system of self-evident ideas and beliefs.

What has rarely been seen is the fact that Mendelssohn, despite the philosophical questions raised by his definition of Judaism, came close to the truth in his feeling that the historical distinctiveness of Judaism has always manifested itself primarily in *Halakha,* a specific way of life guided by a system of law governing ethical conduct and ritual practices. Mendelssohn's position is in harmony with Judaism's persistent aversion to the formulation of creeds and its insistence that man wins merit primarily by his affirmation of God through conduct, not through creed.

Mendelssohn's thinking can be understood only against the background of the causes that command his loyalties. His faith in the power of reason was linked with his passion for human equality and his uncompromising attachment to Judaism. If, as Mendelssohn firmly believed, a knowledge of truth is indispensable to the achievement of man's happiness, truth has to be accessible to all people alike without distinction of race, creed, or social status. It was inconceivable to him to believe that God, in His goodness, could capriciously have revealed the truth only to a part of mankind and left the rest of mankind without revelation and therefore without access to true happiness. No one religion can be the sole instrument through which God has revealed His truth. As he wrote in a letter to Jacob Emden,[3] which is as moving as it is illuminating: "Are we to assume that all inhabitants of the earth, from sunrise to sunset, are condemned to perdition if they do not believe in the Torah which has been granted solely as the inheritance of the congregation of Jacob? . . . What, then, are those peoples to do that are not reached by the radiant rays of the Torah? . . . Does God act like a tyrant when He deals with His creatures, destroying them and extirpating their name, even though they have done no wrong?" Truth is indivisible and must be accessible to all men.

But it was equally impossible for Mendelssohn to surrender his deep attachment to Jewish life. He found emotional and intellectual satisfaction in the observance of Jewish law. It enabled him to perform the acts—the *mitzvot*—that bind him to God and unite him with his people. Above all, such acts safeguard the continued existence of the Jewish people. Therefore, Mendelssohn insisted time and again on the crucial importance of law for the Jew. He even proclaimed boldly that, if a choice has to be made, it is better that the Jew surrender the benefits of emancipation than his loyalty to the law.

Mendelssohn's significance for Jewish life lies in the fact that he was the bridge between the Jewish world and that of Europe. A citizen of both worlds, he managed to bridge them in his own personality. In his thinking, he was a European; in sentiment and conduct, he was anchored in the Jewish community and identified with its traditions.

Through his work and personal example, Mendelssohn also enabled other Jews to bridge the same two worlds. His translation of the Pentateuch prepared the way for the cultural emancipation of Jews by placing the treasures of European culture within their linguistic reach. His writings and the example of his personality helped to pave the road for civic emanicipation as well. As he gained the friendship and admiration of influential Christians, he won allies who associated themselves with the Jewish battle for human rights and created the moral and intellectual climate for the ultimate emergence of Jewish emancipation.

However, Mendelssohn's attempt to bridge the two worlds philosophically as well as culturally and socially did not succeed. His contemporaries and successors were unable to accept his definition of Judaism. They agreed that law—customs and ceremonials—was one of Judaism's vital ingredients. Obviously, however, Judaism is more than a mere system of legal prescriptions. The law itself presupposes a belief in God who has given it, who requires its observance, who is the Master of man's destiny and the Source of all life. This God cannot be "proved" by reason, and therefore the question remains of how the faith of biblical Judaism can be harmonized with the demands of reason and the findings of science.

What makes Mendelssohn important to the modern Jew is not his definition of Judaism but the questions he raised. Standing at the threshold of Jewish modernity in Central Europe, he was the first to formulate the central problems which had begun to trouble his generation and to which, since then, each new Jewish generation has had to find a meaningful answer: how to live as a Jew without surrendering the values of Judaism to the values of the modern world or the wisdom of the world to the claims of Judaism.

Much has been written about Mendelssohn. His own writings, however, and especially his Jewish writings, are available to the English reader only in antiquated translations in virtually inaccessible editions.

For this reason, Mendelssohn's major writings on Judaism are presented here in a completely new translation. The two most characteristic works in which he develops his Jewish position—*Jerusalem* and the *Letter to Johann Caspar Lavater*—are included in full. The remainder of the volume contains selections from other works by Mendelssohn and especially from his extensive correspondence, selected to introduce the reader to all major facets of Mendelssohn's thinking on Judaism—revelation, miracles, Judaism and Christianity, the limitations of religious authority, the meaning of the law, the fundamental principles of Judaism. Since Mendelssohn frequently repeated his arguments or formulations in his voluminous writings and correspondence, several selections were shortened (as indicated by ellipsis dots) in order to eliminate duplication.

ALFRED JOSPE

Washington, D.C.

*JERUSALEM OR
ON RELIGIOUS
POWER AND
JUDAISM*

CHAPTER 1

State and religion, human and divine legislation, secular and ecclesiastical authorities—to establish a balance between these forces so that they will support the structure of society rather than crush its foundations has for centuries been one of the most difficult tasks in political life.

It has usually been easier to solve this problem in practice than in theory. Some people, for instance, have found it advisable to classify these social forces as different moral entities, each possessing a domain of its own with specific rights, duties, powers, and properties. However, neither their respective territories nor the borderlines separating them have, so far, been properly defined. On occasion, we see the church carry its banner far into the territory of the state. The state, in turn, will permit itself encroachments which are equally illegitimate by any accepted standard. Enormous evil has resulted from the clash of these forces; more threatens yet to come. Whenever there is a conflict between these forces, mankind becomes the victim of their quarrels. But even when they are in agreement, the most precious jewel of human happiness is in danger of being lost, for their agreement rarely serves any other purpose than to ban from their realm a third moral force, *freedom of conscience*, which usually knows how to derive some advantage from their disunity.

Despotism has one advantage: it is consistent. Its demands

11

may be onerous in the light of common sense, but they are clear-cut, concise, part of a uniform pattern. It has a definite answer to every question. Never mind its limitations—he who has everything has no need to worry about the cost. The same holds true for the constitution of the church, according to Roman Catholic principles. It covers every aspect of life and is all of one piece, as it were. You may be required to comply with all its demands, but at least you know where you stand. Your house is safely built, and tranquillity reigns in all its rooms. Of course, this tranquillity is merely that dreadful calm which, in Montesquieu's phrase, prevails during the evening in a fortress expecting to be taken by assault during the night. But those who equate happiness with undisturbed calm in doctrine and life will find it nowhere with greater certainty than under a Roman Catholic despot; or rather, because even in this case power is still too much divided [between the ruler of the state and the head of the church], under the despotic rule of the church itself.

But as soon as freedom dares to remove even the smallest structural element in this building, the entire edifice threatens to collapse, and no one knows how much of it will remain standing in the end. This accounts for the extraordinary confusion and disturbance in civil and church affairs that occurred during the first years of the Reformation. It also accounts for the striking embarrassment one could observe among the teachers and spokesmen of the Reformation whenever they had to determine how far to go in granting rights to the masses. It was, of course, difficult to keep the large, newly unfettered masses within the necessary bounds. However, even the theoretical writings of that time are vague and vacillating whenever they attempt to define the power of the church. The despotism of the Roman church was abolished—but what was to take its place? Even now, in our own, more enlightened time, the compendiums of church law remain vague on this point. The clergy will not or cannot relinquish all claims for the right of the church to play a role in the affairs of the state. Yet no one knows what this role should be. Some people seem determined to settle doctrinal controversies without even acknowledging a supreme judge. Others continue to refer to a church that is independent [of the state], yet no one knows where to find it. Still others advance a claim for powers and rights, yet no one can tell you who should exercise them.

Thomas Hobbes lived in a period when fanaticism, coupled with an undisciplined desire for freedom, recognized no bounds and was ready—something which it later accomplished—to stamp out royal power and to overthrow the country's political structure. Weary of civil strife and by nature inclined toward a life of quiet contemplation, he considered tranquillity of mind and security as supreme blessings regardless of how they were to be achieved; and he felt they could not be realized unless undivided power was concentrated in the hands of the sovereign state. Consequently, he thought that public welfare would be best served if everything, even our judgment of right or wrong, were made subject to the supreme jurisdiction and power of the civil authorities. He based this theory on the premise that man is entitled to everything he can get by employing the powers with which nature has endowed him. He claimed that the original state of nature is a state of general anarchy—a war of all against all, in which every man *may* do what he *can* do. Might is right. He felt that this deplorable state of affairs lasted until men agreed to put a stop to their misery, to relinquish rights and powers when they endangered public security, and to place their administration in the hands of a properly constituted authority. Hence, right is now what this authority commands.

Hobbes either was insensitive to the need for civil liberty or else would rather see it abolished than abused. Yet in order to preserve his own freedom of thought—a freedom of which he made more use than anyone else—he resorted to a subtle argument. According to his system, all *right* is grounded in *might*, all *obligation* in *fear*. Inasmuch as God is infinitely more powerful than any civil authority, God's right must also be infinitely superior to that of the human authority. Consequently, our fear of God imposes upon us obligations which must never yield to any fear of human authorities. Interestingly enough, Hobbes felt that this principle applied only to man's private religious beliefs, which were that philosopher's sole concern in this context. However, in all matters of public creed and cult the civil authorities were to have the final word, and he regarded any unauthorized change or innovation in church affairs not only as treason but as heresy. By introducing this kind of subtle distinction, he attempted to avoid a collision between personal religious conviction and public worship. We have to admire the ingenuity with which he tried to make his system consistent, even though the logical gaps which remain reveal the weakness of his approach.

Nevertheless, Hobbes's propositions contain a great deal of truth. The confusion to which they ultimately led was largely the result of the exaggerated formulations which he used out of love for the paradox or in response to the conditions of his time. Moreover, in his time the concept of natural law had not yet been sufficiently clarified. Nevertheless, Hobbes did for moral philosophy what Spinoza had done for metaphysics. His subtle fallacies stimulated further inquiry, with the result that the concepts of right and duty, of authority and obligation, have been defined more adequately since then and people have learned to distinguish more correctly between physical and moral power, between might and right. These distinctions have now become part of our language to such an extent that Hobbes's system seems to be refuted not only by common sense but by the very terminology we are using. The same happens, of course, with regard to every moral truth. As soon as it has become generally known and accepted, it enters into our everyday language and thought to such an extent that it becomes familiar and comprehensible even to the average intellect. We begin to wonder how man could ever have stumbled or erred on what seems to have been so smooth a path; but we forget the painful effort that was needed to clear a trail through the wilderness.

Hobbes himself must have been aware of the untenable consequences and implications of his extreme position. If man is not bound by nature to any duty, there is no reason why he should be under any obligation to keep his contracts. If, in the realm of nature, fear and weakness are the sole reasons for the assumption of obligations, any contract is binding and effective only as long as it is supported by fear and weakness. Consequently, contracts do not bring mankind a single step closer to greater security; men still remain in the primitive state of universal warfare. Contracts will be binding without additional safeguards and agreements only if man does not consider it his natural right to violate a covenant made in good faith. He must not be *permitted* such a violation even if he *can* commit it; he should not have the *moral right,* even though he may have the *physical ability,* to violate a compact. Might and right are clearly different matters, even in the domain of natural law.

To take another issue: Hobbes imposed a strict obligation upon the civil authorities not to demand anything of their subjects which would be detrimental to their welfare. For though the authorities are not accountable to any man for their actions, they do owe an account to the Supreme Judge; and even though, according to Hobbes's principles, the authorities need not feel constrained by fear of any human power, they must feel bound by fear of the power of the Almighty, who has made His will sufficiently known to them. Hobbes was quite explicit on this point. In fact, he was considerably less lenient with the gods of the earth than his system would warrant. At any rate, if the very fear of the Supreme Power is capable of imposing certain obligations toward their subjects upon kings and princes, it can also produce a sense of duty and obligation in every individual. We have another basic natural right here, although Hobbes did not admit it. Today any student of natural law can argue this point successfully with Thomas Hobbes—to whose arguments he owes this very triumph.

Locke, who lived during the same troubled period, attempted to protect freedom of conscience in a different way. In his *Letters on Tolerance,* he defined a state as a society of men who unite and act collectively to promote their temporal welfare. Consequently, the state is not to concern itself with a citizen's convictions regarding his eternal salvation. It must tolerate all whose civil conduct does not interfere with their fellow citizens' pursuit of temporal happiness. The state as state has no right to take no-

tice of the differences between religions, for religion inherently
has no bearing or influence on temporal affairs. Any connection
between the two realms is the result of an arbitrary act of men.

Well then, if the dispute could be settled by a verbal definition, I would know of none that is more convenient; and if words
could have talked the restless minds of his age out of their in-
tolerance, the good Locke himself would not have found it necessary to go into exile quite so frequently. But, his opponents ask,
what prevents us from promoting our eternal happiness collectively too? In fact, on what grounds can we restrict the regulative
power of society merely to the realm of temporal affairs? If men
can promote their eternal salvation by public measures, duty as
well as reason would demand that they band together for this
purpose.

Now, if the state limits its concerns merely to temporal matters, a question arises: To whom are we to entrust the care for the
eternal? To the church? Then we would be back at the point
from which we had started [i.e., the tension between] state and
church, concern for the temporal and the eternal, civil and ecclesiastical authority. Their relationship is the same as that of the
temporal to the eternal. Hence the state is subordinate to religion
and must yield whenever a collision between the two occurs.

But if this were correct, on what grounds can anyone reject
the dreadful implications of Cardinal Bellarmine's arguments
that the head of the church, in order to advance the eternal, also
has jurisdiction over everything temporal;[4] that his sovereignty
extends at least indirectly over all persons and possessions
of the world; that all secular realms are indirectly subject to the
authority of the spiritual ruler; and that they have to follow his
orders if they want to change their form of government, depose
their kings, or appoint others in their stead? He maintains that the
spiritual welfare of the state cannot be guaranteed in any other
way—a doctrine which, together with numerous other maxims
of his order, Bellarmine set forth with great ingenuity in his work
De Romano pontifice. But the numerous objections raised in voluminous works against the Cardinal's fallacious arguments are

really beside the point as soon as the state completely relinquishes its control over man's spiritual concerns.

Actually it is neither correct nor in man's best interest to distinguish so sharply between the temporal and the eternal. Eternity, in principle, can never be man's portion; his "eternity" is merely an infinitely prolonged temporality. His temporality never ceases; it is an integral and essential part of his continuity. To counterpoise man's temporal welfare and his eternal bliss leads to a confusion of concepts which has important practical consequences. It shifts the borders of the sphere in which man can act in accordance with his capabilities and extends his reach beyond the limits which Providence, in her wisdom, has set for him. If I may quote myself here: "on the dark path man has to travel in this life, he is granted just enough light to be sure of his next step. More would only blind him, and any lateral light would merely confuse him."[5] I grant that it may be necessary to remind man continually that all is not over when this life ends and that he must expect a future state of infinite duration for which his life down here is merely a preparation, just as, in all of creation, the present is merely a preparation for what is still to come. As our rabbis say, this life is merely a vestibule in which we are to prepare ourselves if we wish to enter the innermost chamber.[6]

Nevertheless, we must be careful not to establish an antithesis between this life and the one to come or to persuade people that their true welfare in this life and their eternal bliss in the life to come are unrelated—that their temporal and their eternal well-being are two different things and that it is possible to pursue the one while neglecting the other. Such delusions will simply distort the outlook and perspective of the simple-minded person, who will lose his bearing and begin to stumble on what, in reality, is a straight and level road. Far too many people do not dare to enjoy the bounties that Providence bestows on them here and now, for fear of losing an equivalent portion in the hereafter, and some men have deliberately neglected their responsibilities as citizens on earth in the hope of thereby becoming better citizens of heaven.

Several considerations have enabled me to clarify my own thinking about state and religion—their respective limits, their influences upon each other, and their effect upon the pursuit of happiness in civil life. As soon as man recognizes that he can neither fulfill his duties toward himself, his Creator, and his fellowman nor escape the oppressive misery of loneliness if he lives in isolation from society, he has the obligation to end this state of isolation and to associate himself with his peers so that they can assist each other in their needs and promote a common welfare by joint efforts. Their common welfare, however, comprises the present as well as the future, their spiritual as well as their material concerns. They are inseparable. Unless we fulfill our obligations, we can expect happiness neither here nor hereafter, neither on earth nor in heaven. But, for the fulfillment of our obligations, two things are required in turn: action and conviction. "Action" is the realization of what duty demands; "conviction" ensures that our actions spring from proper and correct motives.

Human perfection thus requires both action and conviction, and it is the task of society to promote both vigorously through the collective efforts of all. In other words, society must guide the actions of its members toward the common good, and it must nurture the convictions which will eventuate in such actions. The one, society achieves through government; the other, through education. Man can be induced to submit to both by reasons he considers cogent: he can be prompted to action by proper motivation, and he can be led to conviction by his proper understanding of the truth. Society must therefore promote both through public institutions in such a way that they will cooperate harmoniously for the common good.

Man's rational actions and convictions are determined partly by his relations to his fellowmen and partly by his relations to his Creator and Keeper. The former are the province of the *state*, the latter that of *religion*. Insofar as man's actions and convictions, which serve the common good, spring from the relations between man and man, they are the domain of civil law; where the source of man's actions and convictions is his relationship to God, they are the domain of church, synagogue, and mosque.

Some of the writings that deal with canon law seriously question whether Jews, heretics, or heterodox believers can have a "church" of their own. The question is not quite as absurd as it may appear to the unbiased reader in view of the limitless privileges which the so-called church likes to arrogate unto itself. To me, this terminological distinction does not matter. Those public institutions for the training of man which deal with his relations to God I call "church"; those which deal with his relations to man I call "state." By "training" I mean the attempt to guide man's actions and convictions in such a way that both will jointly promote the well-being of mankind. I mean, in short, the education and government of man.

Happy is the state which succeeds in governing its people by education alone so that they will engage in socially useful acts as a result of their morality and attitudes rather than because they have to be constantly spurred on by the law. As a social being, man must surrender many of his rights for the general good, or, as we can also put it, he must often sacrifice his own advantage to a benevolent concern for others. But he will be happy only when this sacrifice is made of his own volition and when he realizes, each time anew, that he acts solely out of a concern for his fellowmen. Basically, altruism makes us happier than egotism, provided we sense that our action represents a realization of our human potential. Contrary to the claims of some sophists that man is motivated by nothing but self-love, benevolence ceases to be benevolence and has neither value nor merit if it does not flow freely from the benefactor's own volition and initiative.

This consideration can also provide us with a satisfactory answer to the well-known question, Which form of government is the best? Until now, a number of contradictory answers—all of them apparently true—have been given to this question. Actually, the question is too vague, as is a similar question in the medical field, Which food is best for our health? Obviously, each complexion, climate, age, sex, and way of life requires a different answer. The same is true with regard to our politico-philosophical problem. For each people, at each stage of their civilization, a different form of government will be best. Some despotically governed nations would be miserable if they were left to govern themselves. Liberal republicans would be equally miserable if they were subjected to the rule of a monarch. And a nation may actually change its form of government whenever there is a change in its culture, way of life, or mode of thinking. In the course of the centuries, it may thus run the whole gamut of governmental forms from anarchy to despotism, with all their shadings and variants; yet it will always have chosen the form of government that was best suited to the circumstances of the time.

However, I believe that, regardless of circumstances and conditions, there is only one infallible criterion for determining the quality of any form of government. It is the extent to which people are governed by means of education alone, so that government will be the product of moral standards and ethical convictions. In other words, that government is best which enables every citizen most adequately to realize that he must renounce some of his rights for the common good, that he must sacrifice part of his self-interest for the sake of others, and that he will actually gain just as much through his altruism as he will lose through this sacrifice. In fact, his sacrifice will add greatly to his inner happiness inasmuch as it increases the merit and dignity of his act and thus enhances the true perfection of the benefactor. It is, for example, not advisable for the state to take over all humanitarian tasks, including charity, and to assign the responsibility for them to public agencies. Man becomes conscious of his worth and dignity only when he himself performs charitable acts, when he perceives clearly how his gift alleviates the needs of his fellowman, when he gives because he *wants* to give. If he gives only because he *must*, he will be conscious only of the fetters that shackle his will.

One of the state's main efforts must therefore be to govern men by influencing their morals and attitudes. Now, there is no better way of improving the attitudes and thereby the morals of men than a strongly held conviction. Laws do not change attitudes; arbitrary punishments and rewards neither produce a concept of truth nor improve morality. Fear and hope are no criteria for truth, either. Knowledge, reasoning, and conviction alone can generate ethical principles which, by serving as examples that command respect, will ultimately become generally accepted moral criteria for everyone.

And it is here that religion can come to the assistance of the state and the church can become the support of civic welfare. The task of the church is to convince people, with all the emphasis at its command, of the truth of the principles and views it proclaims. The church must show them that duties toward men are also duties toward God and that to reject them is to live in deepest misery. It must show them that by serving the state we truly serve God; that law and justice are the commands of God; that charity is His sacred will; and that the true acknowledgment of the Creator cannot leave even a residue of hatred for our fellowmen in any human soul. To teach this is the charge, duty, and vocation of religion; to preach this is the charge, duty, and vocation of its ministers. It is inconceivable to me how men could ever have permitted religion to teach, and its ministers to preach, exactly the opposite.

If, however, the character of a nation—its cultural development, its growing prosperity, increasing population, excessive luxury, and other conditions and circumstances—makes it impossible to govern the people on the basis of their attitudes alone, the state will have to resort to public measures such as the enforcement of the law by coercion, the punishment of crime, and the rewarding of merit. If a citizen is unwilling to defend his country because he lacks a sense of duty, he will have to be tempted by rewards or compelled by force [to fulfill his obligation]. If men have lost their feeling for the intrinsic worth of justice or if they no longer realize that honesty in word and deed is true happiness, it becomes necessary for the state to correct injustice and punish fraud.

In this way, however, the state attains society's true goal only halfway. External inducements cannot make an individual happy, even though they may affect him to some extent. The man who avoids deception because he loves righteousness is happier than the man who avoids it merely because he is afraid of the arbitrary punishments the state metes out for fraud. To his fellow-man, by way of contrast, it does not matter why the wrong is not committed, or by what means his rights and property are protected. The country will be defended regardless of whether a citizen fights for it out of patriotism or out of fear of punishment —even though the defenders themselves will be happy in the former and unhappy in the latter case. If it is impossible for society to achieve inner happiness, at least it will be possible to bring about external tranquillity and security.

The state will thus be content with mere deeds—with conduct without conviction, with conformity of action without concurrence in thought. Even though a person may have no regard for laws, he must obey them as soon as they have been enacted. The state may grant the individual citizen the right to criticize laws, but not to act in accordance with his criticism. This right a citizen has to renounce as a member of society, for no society can exist without this renunciation.

Not so with religion. It knows no act not founded on conviction, no work without spirit, no deed without inner concurrence, no consensus concerning action without agreement upon its meaning. Religious deeds without religious motivation are empty mechanical motions [literally, "puppetry"], not service of God. Religious deeds must spring from conviction; they can neither be purchased by the promise of a reward nor enforced by the threat of punishment.

Nor is religion concerned with those civil acts that have been motivated by force rather than by conviction. As long as the state exerts its influence only through reward and punishment, it cannot expect any assistance from religion. For as long as this condition exists, man's duties toward God are disregarded, and the relationship between man and his Creator has become inoperative. The only assistance that religion can render the state is through teaching and comforting. It can use its divine teachings to instill ideas in the citizen that are of benefit to the community; and it can bring spiritual comfort to the unfortunate creature who has been condemned to death as a sacrifice to the common good.

Here we have a first essential difference between state and religion. The state commands and coerces, religion teaches and persuades. The state issues laws, religion issues commandments. The state possesses physical power and uses it when necessary; the power of religion is love and charity. The one abandons the lawbreaker and expels him from society; the other draws him close and seeks to instruct or at least to comfort him, not always without profit, even during the last moments of his earthly life. In one word: civil society, viewed as a moral person, has the right of coercion; in fact, it has secured this right through the social contract. Religious society neither demands the right of coercion nor can it possibly obtain it by any contract. The state possesses absolute rights, the church, limited rights. In order to clarify this point, let me go back to the first principles and examine them more thoroughly.

THE ORIGIN OF THE RIGHT OF COERCION AND THE VALIDITY OF CONTRACTS AMONG MEN

I realize I am in danger of becoming too speculative for some of my readers. However, anyone is free to omit what he dislikes. At the same time, it may not be disagreeable to the friends of natural law to see how I tried to define its first principles for myself:

"The faculty (the moral capacity) to use a thing as a means for promoting our happiness is called a *right*. This capacity is called *moral* if it is compatible with the laws of wisdom and goodness. The things which can serve as means to promote happiness are called *goods*. Man, therefore, has a right to certain goods or means of promoting his happiness, insofar as this right is not in conflict with the laws of wisdom and goodness.

"Whatever ought to be done in accordance with the laws of wisdom and goodness (or ought to be omitted as being in con-

flict with these laws) is called *morally necessary*. The moral necessity (obligation) to do, or forgo doing, something is called a *duty*.

"The laws of wisdom and goodness cannot contradict each
other. If I have a right to do something, my fellowman cannot
have the right to prevent me from doing it. Each right, therefore,
has its corresponding duty. The duty to submit corresponds to
the right to act; the duty to comply corresponds to the right to
demand, etc."[7]

Wisdom, coupled with goodness, is called *justice*. The cardinal principle of justice, on which a right is based, either confers
this right on its possessor unconditionally, or it does not. In the
first case it is a *perfect*, in the second, an *imperfect* right. A right
is imperfect when the conditions under which it is granted
may in part remain unfulfilled, depending on the knowledge and
conscientiousness of the person who has to fulfill them. In the
first instance [that of the perfect right], he is completely bound
to the performance of the duty which corresponds to the other
person's right; in the second instance, he is bound to that performance only incompletely.

Accordingly, there are perfect and imperfect *duties* as well
as rights. The first are called *compulsory* rights and *compulsory*
duties; the others, however, are merely *claims* (petitions) and
duties of conscience. Compulsory rights are external to man and
can be exacted by force. Petitions are internal and may be rejected. Failure to fulfill compulsory duties constitutes an offense,
or an injustice; failure to fulfill duties of conscience, however, is
merely an impropriety, or wrong.

The goods to which man has an exclusive right are, first, his
own capacities; second, whatever he produces or improves through
the use of his capacities—what he builds, saves, protects, etc. (the
products of his industry); third, goods of nature which are so
closely interconnected with the products of his efforts that they
cannot be separated from each other without being destroyed
and which he, consequently, has made his own. These last
goods represent his *natural* property. They were excluded from
the original "communality of goods" even in earliest times, long
before mankind developed any social contract. For men originally

possessed in common only those goods which are produced by nature, without man's industry and fostering care. In other words, man's claim to property is not always based merely on a social convention.

Man cannot be happy without beneficence, whether it be passive, through receiving it, or active, through extending it. He cannot attain perfection except through mutual assistance; through reciprocity of service and deeds of kindness; through active and passive involvement with his fellowman.

A person who possesses goods or controls means of happiness which may add to his well-being but are not actually necessary for his existence, is therefore duty-bound to use them at least in part for the benefit of his fellowmen. Well-being and benevolence are inseparable.

Vice versa, he has the same claim on the benevolence of others. He can expect and, indeed, demand that they assist him with the goods they can spare and aid him in his striving for perfection. Let us, however, not forget what we mean when we speak of "goods." The term denotes all inner and outer possessions of man insofar as they can become a means of achieving happiness for him and others. Hence, everything which is his by nature—his industry, his mental capacities, his physical powers, everything which he can call his own—can be used partly for his own benefit (and advantage) and partly for the benefit of others (benevolence).

Our possessions are, however, limited and exhaustible. Therefore, it may happen that the same property cannot be of use to me and my neighbor simultaneously. Consequently, I cannot utilize my property for the benefit of all my fellowmen at all times and under all circumstances. Now, inasmuch as it is my duty to make the best possible use of my possessions and gifts, my course of action will have to depend on the choices I make and on the way I clarify my thinking with regard to questions such as, How much of what I own should I devote to benevolence? For whose benefit? At what time and under what circumstances?

Who is to make these decisions? Who shall adjudicate the collisions of interest [that may arise]? Certainly not my neighbor;

he does not know all the factors and grounds on which this conflict of obligations will have to be resolved. Moreover, every other human being would, in principle, have the same right, and if, as would most likely happen, each of them were to decide to his own advantage, the difficulty would not be resolved.

Consequently, I—and I alone—am entitled by nature to decide whether, when, for whose benefit, to what extent, and under what conditions I am duty-bound to practice benevolence. There is no natural law that could compel me to practice benevolence at any time. My duty to do good is only a duty of conscience, concerning which I am not obliged to render an account to anyone, just as my right to the beneficence of others is merely a right to petition, which can be rejected. By nature, all *positive* duties of men toward each other are merely imperfect duties, just as their positive rights are merely imperfect rights—they are not duties which can be exacted or rights which can be enacted by coercion. Only the duties and rights of *omission* are perfect by nature: I am unconditionally obliged *not* to injure anyone, and I am just as unconditionally empowered to prevent anyone from injuring me. To inflict injuries, however, means, as is well known, to act against the perfect right of another person.

Now, one could assume that the duty to provide indemnification is a positive duty incumbent upon man by nature. If I have injured someone, I am duty-bound, not by contract but simply by the laws of natural justice to indemnify him for the injury. In fact, he can compel me to do so.

However, despite the fact that indemnification is a positive act, the obligation to provide it is basically derived from the negative command, "Do not offend." For the wrong I have inflicted upon my fellowman remains a continuous offense as long as its effects are not eliminated. Properly speaking, I act contrary to a negative duty as long as I fail to provide indemnification, for I permit the offense to continue. Therefore, the duty to indemnify constitutes no exception to the rule that man is autonomous by nature, that is, without positive obligations to anyone. No one is legally entitled to prescribe to me how much of my energy I should devote to the welfare of others or for whose benefit I should expend it. It must be left exclusively to my discretion to determine the criterion by which I want to adjudicate any cases involving a collision of interests.

Nor does the natural relationship of parents and children run counter to this universal law of nature. It would seem clear that persons who can act rationally and judiciously with regard to collisions of interest, can by nature be autonomous. Consequently, children have no claim to self-determination before they reach the age when they can be expected to use their reason. Until then they must let others decide how and for what purposes they are to use their energies and faculties. The parents, on their part, must gradually train their children in the art of making rational decisions whenever a conflict of interests arises and allow them increased freedom and independence in the use of their faculties as their capacity for judgment grows.

Now it is true that parents have, by nature, certain obligations to their children. One could actually define these obligations as a positive duty which can be enforced without requiring a contract, simply in accordance with the eternal laws of wisdom and goodness. Nevertheless, it seems to me that the right of parents to educate their children is by nature theirs alone. It belongs to either parent vis-à-vis the other but to no third party that might wish to take charge of the children and wrest the right to bring them up from their parents. By nature, no one can coerce parents to educate their children, but that the parents themselves can compel each other to do so is *de facto* inherent in their [marital] agreement, even though it may not explicitly state this right in so many words.

Anyone who has shared in the creation of a human being capable of happiness is bound by the laws of nature to promote this happiness, as long as the child is not yet able to take care of his own development. To provide an education is a natural duty, although, admittedly, merely a duty of conscience. But by the very act of procreation, the parents have affirmed their understanding of the obligation to assist each other in their joint discharge of this duty of conscience. In one word, having consummated their marriage through cohabitation, the parents have tacitly agreed to enable the human being they produce to attain the happiness he is meant to achieve—that is, to educate him.

All matrimonial duties and rights are the natural corollary of this principle, so that it is unnecessary to posit, as law instructors like to do, a double principle from which all duties inherent in marriage and domestic life can be deduced. The duty to educate children follows from the agreement to beget them, and the obligation to set up joint housekeeping follows from the joint duty to educate one's children. Hence, marriage is basically nothing but an agreement between persons of different sex to bring forth children. The entire system of their mutual duties and rights rests on this agreement.[8]

However, by making such agreements, man leaves his original state of nature and enters into the state of society (as will be shown in the following pages). Consequently, the duty of parents to educate their children, even though it can, in some respects, be defined as a compulsory duty, is no exception to the previously mentioned law of nature which shows that man is autonomous by nature and that he alone has the right to use his possessions for himself or for the welfare of others, whenever such a conflict of interests arises.

This right constitutes man's natural freedom, which contributes substantially to his happiness. Autonomy, therefore, is an integral part of his natural possessions, which he may use as one of the means to promote his happiness. Anyone who interferes with this right is guilty of an offense against him and commits an obvious injustice. If man is by nature the master of all that is his, he is entitled to the free use of his energies and talents, just as he may freely use their products (that is, the fruits of his labor), as well as their by-products. He alone has the right to decide how much, when, and for whose benefit among his fellowmen he is willing to give away some of the goods which he can spare. His fellowmen have merely an imperfect right to his surplus goods. They have the right to solicit them, while he, as the absolute master, has the duty to set aside a portion of his goods for the benefit of others. At times he may even be obligated to sacrifice for others what he has set aside for his own use, insofar as the practice of altruism contributes more to a person's happiness than egotism does—provided this sacrifice is made voluntarily and on his own initiative.

All of this seems to me established beyond any doubt. But I still want to go a step further. As soon as this autonomous individual has made a decision, any decision, it must be considered valid. Once I have decided in accordance with my natural right, and have duly made known, to whom, when, and how much I wish to leave of what is mine, and my fellowman, whom I have designated as my beneficiary, has taken possession of the gift, my action must be valid and effective if my right of decision is to have any meaning at all. If my declaration has no effect, leaving matters as they are, if it cannot legally effectuate the change I had intended, my presumed right to make such a decision negates itself. Therefore, my decision must have an effect—it must change the legal *status quo*. The goods in question must cease to be mine and become my fellowman's. The result of my action must be that his previously imperfect right has become a perfect right, while my former perfect right has now become an imperfect right. Otherwise my decision would be null and void. Consequently, I can no longer justly reclaim the relinquished goods after our transaction is completed, and if I were to claim them, I would commit an offense by violating my fellowman's perfect right.

This applies just as much to tangible, movable goods that can be passed from hand to hand, as it does to immovable, spiritual possessions, the right to which can be ceded and acquired only by an appropriate declaratory act. The validity of the transaction depends entirely on a declaration of intent, and the actual transfer of movable goods is legally valid only insofar as it is considered a token of an adequate declaration on the part of the giver. The mere transfer as such confers or rescinds no right unless it is accompanied by a token signifying this intent. Even if I place something in my neighbor's hand, I have not yet, for this reason alone, actually granted him legal possession; and if I take something of his into my hand, I have not legally acquired it unless I indicate in some way that I acted with this intent.

But if the transfer itself has validity only as a token, other meaningful signs or tokens may be substituted for it in cases in which an actual transfer of the goods does not take place. Consequently, we can relinquish our rights to immovable or even intangible goods and transfer them to others with the help of adequately intelligible signs.

In this manner, property can be transferred from one person to another. Whatever I have acquired through my own efforts can become another's property if I relinquish it to him, and I cannot take it back from him without committing an injustice.

Just one more step is needed now to establish the validity of contracts on a firm basis.

The right to decide cases involving a collision of interest is, as previously shown, an intangible property of every autonomous person, insofar as it can become the means for the attainment of his happiness. By nature every person has a perfect right, and his fellowman has an imperfect right, to this means of obtaining happiness. However, since the use of this right is, at least in many cases, not absolutely necessary for man's self-preservation, it constitutes a possession which can be dispensed with, one which, as we have shown, can be relinquished and ceded to someone else through an appropriate declaration of intent. Such an action is called a *promise*, and when the *acceptance* of the second party is added to it—that is, when the other party has duly given its assent to this transfer of rights—a contract results. Thus, a contract is nothing but the renunciation, by the one party, and the acceptance, by the other party, of the right to adjudicate conflicts of interest involving certain goods which the promising party does not require.

Such a contract must be kept, as I have demonstrated before. The right of decision, which had previously belonged to me as part of my natural possessions, has become my fellowman's property by virtue of the fact that it was ceded to him. It is his, and I cannot take it away from him without committing an offense. As a result of our contract, the claim which he, like everybody else, could make for the goods subject to my autonomy—insofar as I do not require them for my self-preservation—has been transformed into a perfect right, which he is entitled to secure by force, if necessary. This conclusion is inescapable if my right of decision is to be valid and effective.[9]

I will now leave my speculations. But before returning to my original train of thought, I want to recapitulate the conditions under which a contract is valid and must be kept in accordance with the principles I have just outlined.

(*a*) Caius possesses certain goods (any means for the attainment of happiness, e.g., the use of his natural faculties; the rights to the fruits of his labor and its by-products, or whatever else has become his by right, be it something tangible or intangible, such as privileges, liberties).

(*b*) These goods, however, are not indispensable to his existence and can, therefore, be utilized for benevolent purposes, that is, for the benefit of others.

(*c*) Sempronius has an *imperfect* right to these goods. He, like everyone else, can urgently request, but not legally enforce the request, that they be used for his benefit right now. The right of decision belongs to Caius. It is his and may not be taken away from him by force.

(*d*) Presently, Caius uses his perfect right to decide in favor of Sempronius, and he makes this decision known by adequate signs; that is, Caius makes a *promise*.

(*e*) Sempronius *accepts* it and signifies his assent in an equally meaningful manner.

Caius' promise is herewith effective and operative. The goods which had previously been his personal property have, by this action, become the property of Sempronius. Caius' perfect right has become an imperfect right, just as Sempronius' imperfect right has now become a perfect right, which is legally enforceable. Caius is obligated to keep this legally valid promise. Should he refuse to honor it, Sempronius can use the power of the law to enforce its fulfillment.

It is by such agreements that man leaves his natural state and enters into the state of social interrelations. His own nature urges him to enter into a variety of social contacts in order to transform his still vague rights and duties into something more definite.

Only the savage, like the beast, clings to the enjoyment of the present moment. Civilized man also lives for the future and wants to take into account what the next moment may bring. Indeed, man's procreative urge itself, unless we consider it merely an animal instinct, impels him, as we have seen, toward a social contract which, in some analogical form, can even be found among many animals.

Let us now apply this theory of rights, duties, and contracts to the distinction between state and church which had been our starting point. Both state and church are concerned with man's acts as well as with his convictions—the former, insofar as they involve the relationship between man and nature, the latter, insofar as they involve the relationship between nature and God. Men need each other; they hope for, pledge, and render each other mutual service and favors. Nature has endowed men with a peculiar mixture of strength and weakness, power and need, selfishness and altruism which drives them to enter into social relations with one another in order to obtain greater latitude for the expression of their capabilities and the satisfaction of their needs. Every individual is obligated to use part of his capacities and rights for the benefit of the society to which he belongs. [The questions arise:] Which part? When? And to what purpose?

To answer these questions is a decision which every individual should, in principle, have the right to make for himself. Nevertheless, it may be advisable to limit the right of autonomous decision by a social contract, that is, by a legal agreement that specifies what portion of his rights a person can be compelled to give up for the good of society. The state, or more precisely, its representatives, is viewed as a moral person which has the power to dispose of these rights. Consequently, the state has rights and prerogatives with regard to the property and actions of its citizens. It can give and take, prescribe and proscribe according to law; and since it is concerned solely with men's actions [and not with their motives], it can punish and reward. Externally, I fulfill my duty toward my neighbor when I do what I ought to do, regardless of whether I do it voluntarily or because I am forced to.

If the state cannot achieve its ends and satisfy my needs by appealing to man's inner impulses and convictions, it can achieve them by outward compulsion, making it at the same time possible for my neighbor to satisfy his needs.

Not so the church. Its foundation is the relationship between God and man. God is not a being who needs our good will, demands our assistance, or usurps any of our rights for His use. Nor can His rights ever collide or be confused with ours. False notions of this kind are the result of the fact that we frequently yet erroneously divide our duties into those toward God and those toward man. People assume there is a direct parallel between our duties to God and our duties to man. Just as our sense of duty compels us to make sacrifices for the benefit of our neighbor, we must do the same out of a sense of duty toward God. Men demand service; so does God. My duty toward myself may conflict with my duty toward my neighbor; in the same way my duty toward myself may conflict with my duty toward God.

But this parallelism goes too far. Nobody would openly defend such absurd notions if they were explained to him in plain language. Yet everybody is still saturated with those views; the judgment is poisoned by them, and they have become the source of many of the unjustifiable presumptions and claims which so-called ministers of religion have always permitted themselves to make in the name of the church. The violence and persecution which they have perpetrated, the conflicts, mutinies, and upheavals which they have instigated, the evils which have been practiced in the name of religion by its grimmest enemies, namely, bigotry and misanthropy—they are all the fruits of this miserable sophistry, of a simulated conflict between God and man, between the rights of the deity and the rights of mankind.

There is no subdivision in the system of human duties that could be entitled "Duties Toward God." All of man's duties are obligations to God. Some of them concern us, others our fellowmen. Love of God demands that we ought to love ourselves in every reasonable way; and we must love His creatures, our fellowmen, in the same way in which we are obligated to love ourselves.

The system of our duties is based on two principles: the relation between man and nature, and the relation between creature and creator. One is the domain of moral philosophy, the other, of religion. In fact, for the man who is convinced that natural laws are nothing but the expression of the divine will, both principles coincide, and the moral teachings of reason will be as sacred to him as those of religion. Nor does religion, the relation between God and man, impose duties and obligations upon man that are different [from those demanded by reason]; religion merely gives solemn sanction to them. God neither needs our assistance nor does He ask any service of us.[10] He needs neither the sacrifice of our rights for His own good nor the renunciation of our independence for His advantage. His rights cannot ever collide or be at variance with ours. He only wants what is best for us, what is best for every individual; and this "best" must obviously be logically consistent and free from contradictions.

I believe these notions are so self-evident that one can only wonder how people could ever have thought differently. Yet, men have always acted contrary to what seems to be self-evident. . . .

An obvious consequence of these principles is, I think, that the church has no claim upon our property and possessions nor any right to expect material contributions and sacrifices on our part. Its prerogatives must never be mixed up with ours. In short, the interests of the church can never collide with those of citizens. Consequently, there can be no contract between church and citizen; for all contracts presuppose that there can be conflicts of interest which have to be arbitrated. Yet where no imperfect rights exist, there can be no collision of claims; and where no adjudication of claim and counterclaim is required, no contract is needed.

No contract can therefore endow the church with the right to our property. Its very nature makes it impossible for the church to advance such a claim. The church can never acquire the right to use coercion, nor can its members be compelled to submit to coercion by the church. The sole right of the church is to admonish and to teach, to confirm and to comfort, while the duties of the citizens toward the church are an attentive ear and a willing heart.[11] Nor has the church the right to reward or punish actions. Civil actions are the concern of the state; genuine religious actions, by their very nature, will not be affected by the use of force or the temptation of bribes. They must flow freely from an impulse of the soul. Otherwise they are a meaningless gesture, utterly alien to the true spirit of religion.

But who is to pay the teachers of religion if the church has no property? Who is to support those who preach the fear of God?

I submit that religion and remuneration, teaching virtue and expecting payment, preaching the fear of God and accepting wages, are mutually exclusive. What effectiveness can the teacher of wisdom and virtue expect when he teaches for pay and is for sale to the highest bidder? What influence can the preacher of piety have when he is out for material rewards? "Behold, I have taught you statutes and ordinances, even as the Lord my God commanded me" [Deut. 4:5]. "Just as God taught me without payment," our rabbis comment, "so do I teach you, and so should you teach yours." [12] Payment and wages are so incompatible with the way of life this exalted profession demands, that the slightest inclination toward gain and profit seems to degrade it and to diminish its stature. The desire for wealth which we readily condone in other professions strikes us as avarice and greed in this; at least it quickly tends to degenerate into avarice and greediness among the members of this noble profession because it is contrary to the very nature of their calling. The most that can conceivably be done for them is to compensate them for their time; but to determine the extent of this compensation and to provide it is the business of the state, not of the church. What concern of the church is it to deal with things which must be bought, hired, paid for? Time is part of our possessions, and the man who uses his time for the welfare of the community is entitled to be compensated for it from communal funds. The church itself, however, must not remunerate. Religion must buy nothing, pay nothing, give no wages.

These, I believe, are the dividing lines between state and church as far as they affect man's *actions*. With regard to his *con-*

victions, however, state and church are not so far apart. Here the state has no other means of influencing man than the church has. Both must instruct, teach, encourage, motivate. But neither may reward or punish, employ force or use bribery; for there is no social contract by which even the state could acquire jurisdiction over man's thoughts and convictions. In short, neither benevolence nor force can sway or influence man's convictions. I cannot renounce any of my views out of love for my neighbor, nor can I cede to him any part of my personal judgment or convictions just because I want to do him a favor. By the same token, I must not arrogate to myself a right to his views or try in any way to gain control of them. The right to our own convictions is inalienable and cannot be transferred from person to person. It does not involve any claim to property, possessions, or liberty.

Hence, even the smallest privilege which you publicly grant to your coreligionists or those who share your views is an indirect bribe, while even the smallest freedom of which you deprive the dissident is an indirect punishment. Both have essentially the same effect that a direct reward for agreement or a punishment for opposition has. The authors of some textbooks of canon law who insist that there is a difference between reward and privilege, punishment and restraint, deceive themselves appallingly. The linguist may find these distinctions useful, but they will hardly comfort the miserable wretch who is deprived of his rights as a human being simply because he cannot say "I believe" when he does not believe or because he does not want to be a Moslem with his mouth when he is a Christian at heart. What, in fact, are the limits of privilege and of restraint? A person requires no more than a moderate talent for sophistry in order to stretch and enlarge these concepts until they are so defined as to constitute either happiness or just the opposite—oppression, exile, and misery.[13]

Fear and hope affect man's emotions and desires; rational arguments address themselves to his cognitive faculty. Therefore, you use the wrong approach if you play on a person's fears or hopes in order to induce him to accept or reject certain doctrines. Even if this were not your intention, you will still spoil your chances [of affecting his thinking] unless you keep fear and hope completely out of sight. You simply deceive your own heart, or your heart has deceived you, if you believe that anyone can arrive at truth or that his freedom of thought can remain inviolate if his ratiocination is either rewarded with status and recognition or punished with contempt and poverty. Our notions of good and evil are the instruments that govern our will; our concepts of truth and error are the instruments which our reason uses. The man who wants to influence our reason had better not use the instrument designed for our will; otherwise he will merely act contrary to his own intentions and remove obstacles where he should have erected them, while fortifying the structure which he should have torn down.

What form of government is therefore advisable for the church? None! Who shall have the authority to settle disputes in religious matters? He to whom God has given the ability to convince others. For of what value is any form of government if there is nothing to be governed? Of what use is authority if no one is to be subject to it? What good is a judiciary if no rights or claims are to be adjudicated? Neither state nor church is competent to serve as judge in matters of religion. Society has not given them this right by any contract. I grant that the state must be vigilant, so that no doctrines will be spread which are detrimental to public welfare or which, like atheism or Epicureanism, might undermine the foundations of society. Let a Plutarch or a Bayle[14] question whether a state might not be better off with atheism than with superstition. Let them count and compare the afflictions which have already befallen and still threaten to befall mankind from these sources of misery. What they are doing is basically no different from what a man does when he examines whether a slow fever is more fatal than a sudden one. No person would wish either upon his friends. Similarly, society would do well to let neither fanaticism nor atheism take root and spread. Regardless of whether the body politic is ravished by cancer or consumed by fever, the result is the same: it becomes desperately ill.

But the state, while remaining vigilant, should nevertheless keep a certain distance even in these matters and, with wise moderation, favor only those doctrines on which its true well-being depends. It should not get involved in any doctrinal controversy nor use its authority to decide it; for it would vitiate its own goals if it prohibited investigation or arranged to settle a controversy in any way other than by reasoned arguments. Nor need the state concern itself with every single principle which may be affirmed or rejected by a religious group, be it a dominant creed or a suppressed sect. We are concerned here only with those major principles on which all religions agree and without which happiness is but a dream and virtue ceases to be virtue. Without [faith in] God, Providence, and a future life, love of man is nothing but a congenital weakness, and humanitarianism little more than a chimera into which we try to trick each other so that the simpleton may get into trouble while the quick-witted can enjoy himself at the other's expense.

It is hardly necessary to discuss also the question whether it is permissible to have teachers and priests testify under oath that they subscribe to certain articles of faith. What doctrines could possibly be validated this way? The basic principles which are common to all religions, and which I have already mentioned, are not subject to confirmation by oath. You will have to take the swearer's word that he affirms them; otherwise, his oath is mere sound, empty words tossed into the air. All trust in oaths, and the respect in which they are held, rest on these fundamental principles of morality. If, however, I am asked solemnly to confirm or abjure certain specific doctrines of a particular religion—doctrines which are not essential to man's virtue and well-being, although, in the opinion of the state and its representatives, they are necessary for my own eternal salvation—then I ask, "What right does the state have to probe into man's soul and to force him to confessions which can bring neither comfort nor benefit to society?" This right could never have been granted to the state because all previously mentioned conditions for a contract are missing here. The issue involves neither my property, which I can dispose of or transfer to my neighbor, nor objects of beneficence. Hence, there can be no clashes of interest that have to be arbitrated. How then can the state claim a right which cannot be bestowed by contract or transferred from one person to another by a declaratory act?

To clarify this point further, let us examine under what conditions an oath concerning a person's belief or disbelief has validity. Can the validity of a man's opinions, his agreement or disagreement with principles established by reason, be verified or confirmed by an oath?

Oaths cannot beget any new obligations. The most solemn invocation of God as a witness of the truth cannot grant or abolish a previously existing right nor impose a duty upon the appellant which he would not have been obliged to fulfill even without an oath. Oaths merely serve to awaken a person's conscience that has become dormant and to call his attention to what the will of the Judge of the world demands of him anyhow. Therefore, oaths are intended neither for the conscientious person nor for the confirmed scoundrel. The former ought to be so thoroughly imbued with the truth that he knows without oath or imprecation that God is his witness—of his verbal statements as well as of his thoughts and hidden motives—and that He will not let any transgression of His holy will go unpunished. And as far as the habitual evildoer is concerned, he is a person without a conscience, and "he who spares no man fears no God."

Oaths are therefore merely for the average person, that is, for most of us who in one way or another belong to that group. Oaths are for the weak, undetermined, irresolute people who have principles but do not always follow them. They are for people who are lazy and indolent with regard to the good, though they know and respect it; for men who are prone to yield to every foible and therefore procrastinate and always seem to look for excuses—which they often seem to find. They are for men who want to go through with their decisions but lack determination. They are for those people whose will must be steeled and whose conscience must be prodded. A man, for example, may conceivably hold someone else's property even though he denies this fact before the judge. Yet he may not be evil or determined to commit an injustice. He may simply have used or lost the property and may

now only want to gain time by his denial. The desire for good
in him, which puts up a fight for justice, is probably weakened
gradually and bit by bit until it disappears completely. In such a
case, we must hurry to his assistance, first using this critical moment to transform his procrastination into action, permitting no
further excuses, and then trying to change his heart by an oath
that summons up all the solemn force and emphasis with which
the thought of God as the all-just Judge and Retributor can possibly impress him.

   This is the purpose of an oath. I think it is obvious that people should be required to take an oath only in connection with
matters that involve sense experience. The evidence of the senses
alone enables a man to state, with the certainty that he is disclos-
ing the truth: "This I have seen, heard, spoken, received, given—
or not seen or heard." But a man's conscience is cruelly tortured
by inquiries which probe into his personal convictions and ask,
"Do you believe? Are you convinced? Persuaded? Do you think
so? And, should any doubt be left in the remotest corner of your
heart and mind, say so or God will avenge the abuse of His
name." For heaven's sake, protect tender and conscientious innocence! In the face of such an adjuration, it would suffer the tor-
ment of uncertainty and hesitation even if all it had to do in such
a moment were to quote a theorem from Euclid's first Book.

   The perceptions of our inner senses are seldom so palpable
that our mind has a firm hold on them and can expound them on
demand. Under pressure they will frequently escape our grasp.
Moreover, I may feel certain of something at this instant, yet only
a moment later a tiny doubt may steal, almost unnoticed, into the
recesses of my mind and continue to lurk there. Some fundamental conviction for whose sake I may be prepared to suffer mar-
tyrdom today may appear problematical to me tomorrow. And
should I be asked to put these inner perceptions into words or
symbols or to swear to them in word or sign prescribed to me by
other people, my inner insecurity will be greater still. My neighbor and I cannot possibly use the same words to express the same
feelings, for we cannot juxtapose, compare, and examine them
again except by words. Words cannot be defined or illustrated by

things. Instead, we must again take recourse to signs, words, and finally, to metaphors. Only by this device can we relate our internal conceptions to the external perceptions of our senses. Clearly, there will always be an enormous amount of confusion and vagueness concerning the meaning of words, and the ideas which different people in different ages associate with the same signs and words will always differ enormously.

Dear reader, whoever you may be, do not accuse me of skepticism or of a reprehensible ruse by which I want to turn you into a skeptic. I am probably among those who are farthest removed from this sickness of the soul, and I fervently wish I could cure my fellowmen of it. But precisely because I have so often attempted to cure myself as well as others of the disease of skepticism, I have become aware of how difficult the job is and that one must not expect easy success. It has frequently happened that I could not agree even with my best friend on certain philosophical and religious truths, although I believe our thinking was perfectly in accord. After considerable controversy and debate we would discover that we had meant different things, even though we had used the same words. We often thought the same way, yet expressed ourselves differently; and just as often our minds were actually far apart, although we thought we were in agreement. This happened even though philosophically both of us were not untrained, were experienced in dealing with abstract concepts, and were far more interested in discovering the truth than in being right. Nevertheless, there was a good deal of friction between us before our ideas would mesh and before we could say with assurance: here we agree. O, I should not like to have for a friend a man who, though he had this experience in his life, can still be intolerant or hate his neighbor for expressing himself differently or for thinking differently in religious matters. Such a man has stripped himself of his humanity.

And you, my fellowmen! You take a man with whom you have probably never discussed such matters, place before him, in symbols and other forms, the most subtle doctrines of metaphysics and religion in the terminology used centuries ago, and make him swear, by the holiest name, that he means by these words exactly what you mean and that both of you think as the man did who wrote these terms down centuries ago. You make him swear an oath that he affirms these principles with all his heart and does not doubt any of them, and then you make this sworn assent the precondition for his attainment of public office and honors, of power and influence—notwithstanding the fact that their lure and enticement can easily silence any man's inner scruples and doubts. Yet should it turn out in the end that his convictions are not what he had professed them to be, you charge him with perjury, the most heinous of crimes, and punish him severely. To put it mildly, are not both sides at least equally guilty in such a case?

"But," the more fair-minded among you may say, "we do not require an oath in matters of faith. We allow freedom of conscience. It is only when we appoint one of our fellowmen to an office which is entrusted to him on the condition that his views conform with ours, that we implore him not to accept the appointment unless he can meet this condition. We simply enter into a contract with him. Should he later begin to have doubts that would make it impossible for him to maintain this conformity, he is free to be faithful to his conscience and to resign. Is there any freedom of conscience or human right that would permit him to break a contract?"

Very well! It would be an unnecessary repetition to enumerate all the arguments one could use against this pretense of justice in accordance with the self-evident principles I have already mentioned. For humanity's sake, however, consider what the results of such a procedure are even among the most moral people. Count all the men who accepted your academic chairs and pulpits but who, later, have come to doubt many of the principles they swore to when they took office. Count the bishops sitting in the Upper House, count all truly great men who hold high office and occupy positions of honor in England but can no longer unconditionally accept the Thirty-nine Articles which they had initially affirmed under oath. Count them all—and then tell me that it is not feasible to grant civil rights to my oppressed people because so many of them have little regard for an oath! Alas, may God protect my heart from misanthropic feelings. They might easily get out of control at these melancholic thoughts.

My respect for humanity persuades me that these men do not think that what they are doing involves them in perjury. Common sense probably tells them that no one, neither state nor church, has the right to require an oath of them in matters of faith, or to make office, honors, or rank dependent on their belief in specific doctrines and their willingness to affirm them by oath. They probably consider such a stipulation to be null and void because it would benefit no one's property rights even if it were broken.[15] If therefore a wrong has been committed—which these men do not deny—it happened because at that moment they were enticed, by the advantages promised to them, to take an oath they considered invalid.

After it has happened, however, it is too late to do anything about it. We certainly cannot ask them to resign the office they secured this way. Granted that initially they had used God's holy name in an indefensible manner in order to secure legitimate material advantages. But once this has been done, it cannot be undone by forcing these men to relinquish the privileges they now enjoy. A bad thing would merely be made worse by the upheaval and scandal which would be the consequence of their resignation and of the public disclosure of their error. The wisest course of action for their fellow citizens as well as for themselves and their associates will therefore be to let matters rest and to continue to serve state and church with the dedication and skills with which Providence has blessed them. Their qualification for public office is based on these factors and not on their views about eternal verities and ethical principles that are no one's business but their own. I realize there are some individuals whose conscience will not permit them to seek their good fortune with the help of such subtle rationalizations, but those who are weak enough to yield to them should not be condemned too severely for it. I, for one, would charge these men only with human weakness, not with perjury.

As a conclusion to this section, let me recapitulate the results of my reflections.

State and church are intended to promote human happiness in this life and in the next, through public arrangements and institutions.

Both influence man's convictions as well as their application. The state affects the relationship between man and man or between man and nature; the church, the state religion, affects the relationship between man and God. The state treats man as the immortal child of the earth; religion treats him as the image of his Creator.

Principles are free. Convictions, by their very nature, cannot be influenced by coercion or bribe. They belong in the realm of man's cognitive power. Their only criterion is whether they are true or untrue. Good and evil, on the other hand, are related to man's capacity for approval or disapproval. Fear and hope guide his impulses. Reward and punishment direct his will; they spur his initiative, encourage, tempt, or deter him.

If principles are to make us happy, they must never be the result of outside pressures or wheedling. The sole criterion by which their validity is to be judged is their rationality. To use any other criterion, to mix it up, for instance, with notions of good and evil, is to invite an unauthorized judge to make the decision.

Thus, neither church nor state has the right to impose any restraint upon man's principles and convictions or to make his status, rights, or claims contingent upon these principles and convictions. Nor may they use any other foreign criterion that might interfere with his cognitive power and weaken his understanding of the truth.

Not even a social contract can grant this right to the state or the church. A contract involving things which by their very nature are inalienable is self-contradictory and *ipso facto* void.

No oath can possibly change this fact. Oaths do not engender new responsibilities; they are simply solemn affirmations of those obligations which we are duty-bound by nature or contract to fulfill in any case. An oath which does not involve any responsibility is a useless and perhaps even blasphemous invocation of God's name. It certainly cannot be binding in any way.

Moreover, men can swear only to what can be supported and

verified by the evidence of their senses—to what they have seen, heard, touched. Thoughts, intellectual perceptions, however, can never be verified by oath.

To abjure or adjure any principles and doctrines is therefore inadmissible. But even if we have done either, we are still not obligated to anything save regret for the unforgivable lack of prudence with which we have acted. If I were to swear to a certain opinion this very moment, I would be afraid to disavow it a moment later. Furthermore, I have merely sworn a meaningless oath even if I retain my opinion; but I have not committed perjury even if I change it later.

We must not forget that, according to my principles, the state is not authorized to make a person's income, position, or status contingent upon his affirmation of specific doctrines. Teachers, for instance, should be appointed solely in accordance with their ability to teach wisdom and virtue and to disseminate the basic verities upon which the well-being of society is founded. In all other matters, however, teachers should be free to act in accordance with their knowledge and conscience. Otherwise, endless confusion and conflict would ensue, until finally even a man of virtue might find himself in a position in which he is tempted to yield to hypocrisy or to betray his conscience. The rules of reason cannot be broken with impunity.

But, you may ask, what happens if a teacher whom the state employs and pays because he holds certain convictions, discovers later that his views are unfounded? What should he do? How can he extricate himself from the trap into which his misguided conscience has led him?

Three courses of action are open to him. He can lock the truth in his heart and continue to teach the untruth against his better knowledge; he can resign from his position without giving any reason; or he can disclose the truth publicly and leave it to the state to determine whether he should retain his job and salary or what consequences he might have to suffer for his indomitable love of truth.

None of these three options, it seems to me, should be rejected completely or under all circumstances. I can conceive of certain conditions under which a man could find forgiveness before the seat of the all-just Judge, if he continued to mix an untruth, perhaps erroneously sanctioned by the state, with the beneficial truth he generally teaches. At least, I have become careful not to accuse an otherwise righteous teacher of hypocrisy or Jesuitry, unless I know the circumstances of the case and his character exceedingly well—and no man can possibly ever know his fellowman's state of mind completely. The man who boasts he has never said anything that differed from what he thought, either never thought at all or simply finds it advantageous to try to impress you with a statement which in his heart he knows to be untrue.

As far as basic convictions and principles are concerned, religion and state are in agreement that both must avoid any semblance of coercion or bribe and that they must confine themselves to instruction, admonishment, persuasion, guidance. However, they differ with regard to actions. The relationship between man and man involves acts as such; the relationship between God and man involves acts only insofar as they are conducive to stimulating the growth of conviction. An act designed to promote the common welfare is no less beneficial for having been enforced; but a religious act is religious only to the degree to which it is performed voluntarily and with proper intent.

Consequently, the state may compel its citizens to act in ways that will promote the common good. It can reward and punish, grant offices and bestow honors. It can admonish or shame people into actions of whose intrinsic value they would otherwise not be aware. For this reason it is possible, and in fact, necessary to grant the state the right as well as the power to use compulsion. Hence, the state must, by social contract, be defined as a moral person, capable of exercising rights and holding property with which it can do as it pleases.

Divinely inspired religion is something utterly different. It does not separate act from conviction in the same way in which the state does. For religion, an act is the expression of conviction. Religion is a moral person, too, but its rights cannot be enforced by coercion. It does not prod men on with an iron rod; it guides them with the gentle hand of love. It draws no avenging sword, dispenses no worldly goods, arrogates unto itself no right to earthly possessions, and makes no claim to legal power over any person's mind. Its sole weapons are reason and persuasion; its strength is the divine power of truth. The punishments it threatens as well as the reward it promises are but manifestations of love —salutary and beneficial to the person who receives them. It is by these signs that I recognize you, daughter of God, religion, who alone, in truth, are all-saving on earth as well as in heaven!

The right to banishment and expulsion which the state may occasionally allow itself to exercise is diametrically opposed to the spirit of religion. To banish, exclude, reject the brother who wants to participate in my devotions and who, together with me, wants to commune with God and find relief for his burdened heart? If religion must not permit itself to deal out arbitrary punishment, it should not permit this torture of the soul which, alas, is felt only by a truly religious person. Think of all the unfortunates, dear reader, who were banished or excommunicated through the ages—supposedly for the improvement of their character! To whatever organized religion you might belong—church, synagogue, or mosque—see if you will not discover more genuine religion among the large number of people who were banished than among the far larger number of those who banished them.

Now, excommunication by the church either has civil consequences or it has none. If it has and excommunication, therefore, brings misery and privation in its wake, it will burden only the noble person who thinks he owes this sacrifice to divine truth. A man who has no religion would be insane if he exposed himself to any danger for the sake of a supposititious truth. On the other hand, if a ban has merely spiritual consequences, as many people like to think, it would have an adverse effect only upon a person who is still sensitive to things spiritual. The irreligious man mocks this sort of thing and remains unaffected and impenitent.

At any rate, how can anyone possibly claim that excommunication has no civil consequences? To grant the church disciplinary power, as I have said elsewhere and, I think, with justification—to grant the church the right to punish without, at the same time, violating a person's civil rights—is similar to the injunction of the supreme Judge to the prosecutor [i.e., Satan]: "I put him into your hands but spare his life" [Job 2:6]. To which the commentators add, "Break the barrel, but don't let the wine run out"![16] What ban or excommunication by the church can possibly be without civil consequences, without adverse influence upon the respect in which a citizen is held, upon the reputation he enjoys, upon the trust his fellow citizens place in him—factors without which no one can pursue his career or be useful to his fellowman and be happy as a citizen?

Yet some people still claim that their rejection of these views is supported by natural law. They maintain that every society has the right of expulsion. Why should a religious society not have the same right?

My answer is that it is precisely with regard to this issue that a religious society is different. There is a higher law which allows no society to exercise a right which is diametrically opposed to its primary purpose. As a respected clergyman of this city [i.e., Berlin] put it, to expel a dissident from the church is like denying a sick person admission to a pharmacy. In fact, the essential purpose and intent of religious societies are mutual edification and spiritual growth. By the miraculous power of mutual sympathy and shared experiences they seek to transfer truth from the mind to the heart and to vitalize, through participation in the experience of worship, a frequently cold and lifeless rational insight. And should the heart be too attached to sensuous pleasures to listen to reason, should it be at the point of ensnaring reason itself, hopefully it may in a religious society learn to recoil from the horror of godlessness and, aflame with the fire of devotion, already come to know on earth the higher joys that provide a balance to mere sensuous pleasures.

Would you really want to turn away from your door the sick person who is most in need of medication, who, in fact, needs it more, the less he is aware of his condition and the more he imagines himself, in his irrationality, to be well? Should not your first concern rather be to restore to him the awareness [of his condition] and to revive the part of his soul which, so to speak, is threatened with gangrene? Instead, you refuse him all assistance and let the powerless soul die a moral death from which you could conceivably have saved him.

How much nobler and more in accord with the goals of his school did the sage of Athens act! Once an Epicurean came from his revelry, his senses befogged by nocturnal debauchery, his head wreathed in roses. He entered the hall of the Stoics early in the morning in order to treat himself to the last pleasure of degenerated gluttons—the pleasure of scoffing. The sage disregarded him but doubled the fiery eloquence with which he was attacking the enticements of dissipation, and he described the bliss of virtue with irresistible force. Epicurus' disciple listened; his attention was caught; he lowered his eyes, tore the garlands from his head, and from then on became a follower of the Stoa.

CHAPTER 2

On a different occasion I have already tried to set forth the most essential aspects of the position which I am taking here and which is radically at variance with a generally accepted principle. It was Mr. von Dohm's excellent essay, "The Civil Improvement of the Jews,"[17] which had originally induced me to examine whether and to what extent a newly established colony should be granted legal autonomy in the administration of its ecclesiastical and civil affairs and, especially, whether it should have the right of excommunication and expulsion.

If a colony is to have legal power in ecclesiastical matters and the right to excommunicate, it must have received them from the state or the mother church. Someone who possesses this right by virtue of a *contrat social* must have ceded and delegated at least part of it to the colony. But what if in principle no one can possess such a right? What if neither state nor mother church has the right to use coercion in religious matters? What if according to the canons of common sense, whose divine origin all of us must acknowledge, state and church can claim no right in matters of faith except the right to teach, no power except the power of persuasion, no discipline except the discipline of reason?

If this position can be shown to rest on evidence that is convincing to common sense, neither a special contract nor tradition nor past usage can have the power to validate a claim which goes against common sense. On the basis of this premise, religious coercion will become unlawful, and the use of compulsion in religious matters will be recognized as a flagrant usurpation of power, inasmuch as the mother church cannot possibly confer a right which it never possessed or give away a power that it had unlawfully arrogated unto itself. It may well be that, as a result of widespread ignorance and prejudice, this malpractice has become so universal and deeply rooted in the hearts of men that it would not be feasible or advisable to abolish it suddenly and completely, without careful and prudent preparation. Nevertheless, it remains our duty to correct it in every possible way and to erect a dam against its further expansion. Even if we cannot wipe out an evil completely, we should at least cut it off from its roots.

This was the result of my reflections, which I ventured to present to the public for its judgment and consideration,[18] even though at that time I could not develop my views as fully as I have done in the preceding section.

I have the good fortune to live in a country in which my ideas are neither new nor particularly striking. The wise sovereign ruling it has from the beginning of his reign made it his goal to grant men their full rights in matters of faith. He is the first among the rulers of this century who has never lost sight of the implications of the wise maxim, "Men have been created for each other; educate your fellowman, or tolerate him!" [19] With wise moderation he has protected the privileges which, as he discovered, had been granted to institutionalized religion. It will probably still take centuries of growing enlightenment before men will understand that privileges based on allegiance to a particular religion are neither legal nor useful and that it would, therefore, be a blessing if all civil distinctions made in the name of religion were unconditionally abolished. In the meantime, however, our nation, under the guidance of this wise ruler, has already achieved so much tolerance and compatibility in matters of faith that the use of religious coercion and excommunication is no longer popularly welcomed.

What must bring special joy to the heart of every righteous man is the seriousness and sincerity with which several leading members of the local clergy [i.e., in Berlin] seek to promote these principles of reason or, more correctly, of true piety among our population. Some of them have actually not hesitated to associate themselves with my arguments against the universal idolization of church rights and to endorse my conclusions publicly. How high must be the regard in which these men hold their vocation if they are willing to disregard the pressures of opposing interests! How strong must be their confidence in the power of truth if they dare to exalt it publicly and forthrightly! Even though we differ substantially with regard to our basic principles, I cannot help but express my respect and wholehearted admiration for their lofty views.

Other readers and literary critics, however, reacted rather strangely. To be sure, they did not contest my arguments. They actually accepted their validity. No one tried to demonstrate that there can or should be the slightest relationship between a person's religious convictions and his legal status. No one found fault with my conclusion that my affirmation or rejection of certain eternal verities entitles me neither to any possessions nor to the authority to use other people's possessions or minds as I please. Yet they were as startled by my conclusions as if they had encountered a sudden apparition. "Does the church have no right whatsoever?" they ask. "Is everything that has been written by numerous authors, including ourselves, about the rights of the church—everything we have said, read, heard, and discussed— completely without foundation?" This, they felt, was going too far. Hence there had to be some hidden error in my reasoning. Otherwise, my conclusions would necessarily have to be correct.

The reviewer in the *Göttingische Anzeigen* first quotes my assertion that no tangible or intangible rights can be derived from a person's religious convictions and that no contracts or agreements between men can produce such a right; but then he adds, "All of this is new and harsh. Where first principles are negated, all discussion has come to an end."

First principles, though not recognized as such, are indeed at stake. But does this mean that all discussion and controversy have therefore ended? May principles never be doubted? If this were the case, the members of the Pythagorean school of thought might have to argue forever *how* their teacher happened to get his golden hip, unless and until someone dares to investigate *whether* Pythagoras actually did have a golden hip.

Every game has its rules, and every contest has regulations which guide the umpire in his decisions. If you want to take the prize or win the trophy, you must abide by the rules. But if you want to study or analyze the theory of games, you have every right to question the ground rules themselves.

The same is true in cases that are before a court of criminal law. Once, a judge who had to try a murderer succeeded in getting him to confess his crime. However, the despicable wretch insisted that he knew of no reason why it should not be just as permissible to murder a man as it is to kill an animal, as long as it is to one's advantage. Hence the judge was obviously justified in telling this subhuman creature, "Since you deny all fundamental principles, you rascal, all further arguments are useless. But you will at least recognize that we, too, are permitted, for our own good, to rid the earth of a monster like you." This kind of answer could, of course, not have been given by the priest who was to prepare the criminal for his execution. His obligation was to discuss the basic principles with the criminal and to help him overcome whatever doubts he might have had concerning them.

The arts and sciences provide us with still another illustration. Each of them starts from certain principles, from premises which require no further proof or justification. Nevertheless, there is not a single point in the totality of human knowledge that can, in principle, be exempt from investigation. Not one iota may escape examination. If a particular court of scholarly adjudication is not competent to deal with my doubts, I must be referred to another court. Somewhere I must be heard and guided in the right direction.

The example which my critic uses in order to refute me completely misses the point. He says, "Let us apply the [author's doubtful] principles to a specific case. Let us assume that the Jewish community of Berlin appoints a person to circumcise its male children according to the laws of its religion. His contract entitles him to a certain income and rank in the congregation. However, after a while he begins to entertain doubts about the doctrinal and religio-legal aspects of circumcision and refuses to fulfill his contractual obligations. Is he still entitled to the rights and benefits he acquired by his contract? The same question applies everywhere."

What does "everywhere" mean? I admit that such a case is possible, though I hope it will never occur.[20] What is this example supposed to prove? Surely not that, according to reason, rights to property or persons depend upon the affirmation of certain doctrines and that specific laws and contracts can validate such a right. These are the two points on which my critic places particular emphasis. Yet neither is applicable to the case he has construed. The circumciser enjoys his income and rank not because he affirms and endorses a specific doctrinal position but because he performed an operation in lieu of the head of the family. Should his conscience keep him from performing this task later on, he must indeed give up the emolument for which he had asked under the terms of the original agreement.

But what does this problem have to do with the privileges granted to a person because he assents to one or the other doctrine or because he accepts or rejects this or that eternal truth?

The only case which might have some similarity to the fictitious situation which my critic has construed is where the state employs and pays teachers who are expected to indoctrinate their pupils in a clearly prescribed specific view but who later feel conscience-bound to deviate from these prescribed doctrines. This case, which I have already discussed in the preceding section and in accordance with my principles, has been the cause of many vociferous and hot disputes. But it really does not seem to fit the quoted illustration. The reader may recall the distinction I made between acts which are required as such, and those which are merely meant to serve as symbols of inner convictions. A foreskin is cut regardless of what the circumciser may believe or think of the custom, just as a creditor for whom the court obtains satisfaction, is paid regardless of what the debtor may think of his duty to pay.

But how can this consideration be applied to the teacher of religious truth whose efforts will be futile unless he teaches with his heart and mind and out of inner conviction? I have already mentioned that I would not dare to tell a teacher in such a predicament how to behave as a man of integrity; nor would I reproach him if he did not resign from his post. The decision, as I see it, depends on the time, circumstances, and conditions in which he finds himself. Who may judge his fellowman's conscience in such a situation or force him to use a criterion which he may not consider appropriate for such a critical decision?

However, this analysis is neither germane to my topic nor relevant to the two questions which are central to the issue under discussion and which I want to restate once more:

(*a*) According to the laws of reason, can rights to persons and things be linked to a person's assent to specific doctrines, or can they be acquired by agreement with them?

(*b*) Can contracts and agreements produce perfect rights as well as compulsory duties unless imperfect rights and duties of conscience had previously existed without any contract?

If my critic wants to prove that I am wrong, he will have to show that at least one of these propositions is valid in accordance with the principles of natural law. The fact that some people consider my proposition new and harsh is irrelevant as long as it cannot be shown that it contradicts truth. For that matter, I do not know of a single author who has touched upon these questions or has examined their possible application to ecclesiastical power and the right of excommunication. They all start from the premise that there is a *jus circa sacra* ["a right inherent in holy things"], but each of them formulates this right in a different way and ascribes it sometimes to an invisible and sometimes to one or the other visible personage. Even Hobbes, who dared to move farthest away from traditional concepts, was not able to free himself completely from this notion. He admits that there is such a right and merely looks for a person to whom it can be entrusted with the least harm. Everybody believes the meteor is visible and, with the help of various systems, merely tries to calculate its distance from the earth. Yet it is quite possible that an unbiased person of far less competence, as he scans the place in the sky where the meteor is supposed to appear, will discover the real truth, namely, that no meteor can be seen anywhere at all!

Let me now proceed to a far more important objection which has been raised against my position and which actually is the primary reason for this essay. Without refuting my arguments, people claim that my views contradict the sacred authority of the Mosaic religion which I profess. What are the laws of Moses, they ask, if not a system of religious government, of religious power and rights? In this connection, an anonymous author says,[21]

> Reason may claim that all church rights and the power of an ecclesiastical court to enforce or limit certain views are unfounded and untenable; that one cannot conceive of any case or situation that would justify such a right; and that not even man's ingenuity and artistry can create anything that does not have its origin in nature. Nevertheless, no matter how rational everything you say may be

he says, addressing me directly,

> it still contradicts the faith of your fathers as well as the principles of your church, which were not simply promulgated by the [post-biblical] commentators but are specifically laid down in the Books of Moses themselves. According to common sense, there can be no true worship without religious conviction; any worship that is the result of compulsion ceases to be worship. The observance of divine commandments out of fear that their infraction will bring punishment is a slavery which clearly cannot be pleasing to God. Nevertheless, it is true that Moses prescribes coercion as well as definite punishment for the nonobservance of ritual duties. His statutory canon, for instance, decrees death by stoning for the man who violates the Sabbath, blasphemes the divine name, or transgresses against Moses' law in other ways.

And he adds elsewhere that

> the entire ecclesiastical system of Moses consisted not merely of teaching and instructing in duties; it was a complete structure of strict ecclesiastical laws. The arm of the church wielded the sword of the curse. "Cursed be he who does not obey all the

words of this law to do them," etc. [Deut. 27:26].²² The implementation of this curse was put into the hands of the highest servants of the church. Clearly, ecclesiastical law armed with coercive power has always been one of the cornerstones of the Jewish religion and a principal article in the religious system of your fathers. How then can you, my dear Mr. Mendelssohn, continue to adhere to the faith of your fathers yet shake its entire structure by removing its very foundation with your denial of the ecclesiastical law that was given by Moses and purports to have been divinely revealed?

This objection goes right to my heart and troubles me deeply. I must confess that this view of Judaism, except for the carelessness of some formulations, is shared by many of my coreligionists. If I were convinced that it is true, I would retract my statements despite the inevitable embarrassment I would have to face, and I would subordinate reason to the yoke of faith. But why play the hypocrite? Authority can humiliate but not enlighten; it can suppress reason but not shackle it. If such an obvious contradiction between the word of God and my own reason actually existed, I would probably be able to silence my reason. Nevertheless, my unresolved questions would continue to perturb me in the recesses of my heart. They would gradually turn into doubts, and the doubts would resolve themselves into childlike prayers and fervent supplications for enlightenment. I would call out with the psalmist, "Lord, send me your light, your truth, that they may guide me to your holy mountain, the dwelling place of your presence" [Ps. 43:3].

In any event, it is not only a distressing but an offensive accusation by the anonymous "Searcher for Light and Right" as well as by Mr. Mörschel (who does identify himself and who has added in a postscript to this "scholar's" essay) that it is my odious intention to abolish the religion I profess and to renounce it covertly, if not overtly. Such hasty inferences and conclusions are inadmissible among scholars. Not everyone who is committed to a certain view is prepared to agree with every conclusion that someone else draws from it, no matter how correct it may seem to be. Such imputations are hateful and merely tend to create bitterness and strife, a situation from which truth rarely emerges as winner.

Indeed, the "Searcher" goes so far as to address me in the following words:

> Is it possible that the remarkable step you have now taken could actually be a step toward doing what Lavater had previously invited you to do? Moved by his appeal, you must undoubtedly have felt inclined to give further thought to the subject of Christianity and, with the careful impartiality and integrity of a searcher after truth, to weigh the value of the Christian systems of religion which you see before you in their various forms and modifications. Do you perhaps feel closer to the Christian faith now, since you seem to have freed yourself from the servitude of the iron bonds of your own church and to have begun to teach the freedom of a more rational religious system characteristic of Christian worship—a system that has enabled us to escape from the coercion of the law and its burdensome ceremonies and that has taught us that true worship of God must not be confined to Samaria or Jerusalem but that the essence of religion is found, in the words of our teacher, "wherever a truly devout person worships God by his commitment to reason and truth"?

This challenge is stated solemnly and movingly enough. Nevertheless, my dear sir, shall I take this step without first pondering whether it will really extricate me from the state of confusion in which you think I find myself? If it were true that the cornerstones of my house are so out of alignment that the entire building threatens to collapse, would I act wisely if I attempted to save my belongings simply by moving them from the lower to the upper floor? Would I be safer there? Christianity, as you know, is built upon Judaism and would therefore collapse along with it. Thus, when you say that my conclusions undermine the foundations of Judaism and offer me the safety of your upper floor, must I not suspect that you mock me? Surely, the Christian who seriously desires to discover light and right will not challenge the Jew to a fight when their respective truths seem to clash or scripture seems to contradict reason. On the contrary, he will join him in an effort to discover the baselessness of the contradiction. For this is their joint concern. The discussion of their doctrinal differences ought to be postponed until later. Their most important task right now is to join forces to ward off the danger that threatens both of them. They must either discover the fallaciousness of their reasoning or demonstrate that they had merely been troubled by an apparent contradiction.

In this way I could, without further discussion with the Searcher, avoid the trap he has set for me. But what would be the advantage of such a subterfuge? Mr. Mörschel, his fellow critic, knows my game only too well, though he does not know me personally. Criticizing my preface, he claims to have detected certain indications which prove to him that I am just as remote from the religious tradition into which I was born as I am from that which he received from his fathers. To prove this assumption, he quotes several of my passages, for instance, where I speak of pagans, Jews, Moslems, and adherents of natural religion in one breath, asking tolerance for all of them. He also quotes the passage where I once again advocate tolerance for the followers of natural religion. Above all, however, he bases his assumption on a quotation where I speak of the eternal verities which religion should teach: "Reason's house of worship has no need of locked doors. Inside there is nothing that must be guarded, and no one who is outside should be prevented from entering. Whoever wants to be a quiet spectator, or even a participant, is, to the devout, most welcome in his house of edification." Mr. Mörschel seems to feel that no true believer in revelation can possibly plead so earnestly for tolerance for the believer in natural religion or speak so freely of eternal verities which religion ought to teach. For him, a true Christian or Jew should have great reservations about calling his house of prayer "reason's house of worship."

I fail to understand what may have put such ideas into Mr. Mörschel's head. Nevertheless, I realize they are the basis of his assumptions and motivate him, as he says, not to ask me to profess the religion he professes or to refute it if I feel unable to convert to it, but to beg me, in the name of all who have the cause of truth at heart, to take a clear and definite stand in matters of such supreme importance to mankind. His intention, he assures us, is not to convert me; nor does he want to give me an opening to raise objections against the religion of which he expects contentment in this life and unlimited happiness thereafter. Nevertheless, he would like to—well, how can I possibly know everything this good man may or may not like?

Let me, therefore, first reassure my kindhearted correspondent by saying that I have never publicly contested the Christian religion and that I shall never enter into a dispute with its true adherents. And to forestall other accusations, namely, that by this declaration I mean to hint at the existence of powerful arguments with which I could refute his faith if I wanted to, or that the Jews possess secret information and still unknown documents which throw a different light on the historical facts as they are usually presented by the Christians, or that I am capable of other deceptions which have always been imputed to us—I say, in order to remove any suspicion of this kind once and for all, I herewith publicly testify that I have nothing new to say against the Christian faith. To the best of my knowledge, we have no information about historical facts and possess no documents other than those which are universally known. For my part, therefore, I have nothing to say that has not already been said countless times by Jews and by the adherents of natural religion and that has not also been repeatedly answered by our opponents. It seems to me that throughout the centuries and especially in our own century, with its abundance of prolific writers, more than enough has been said in this matter. Inasmuch as the parties have nothing new to say, it is time to close the books. He who has eyes will see; he who has discernment will study the issues and then live according to his conviction. What sense does it make for the well-armed champions of this cause to continue to stand by the wayside, challenging every passer-by to battle? Excessive talk about a problem does not clarify it; it merely threatens to obscure the faint glimmer of truth that may remain. Take any subject you please and talk, write, or argue about it—for or against it, often and long enough—and you may be sure that it will gradually lose whatever clarity it may initially have possessed. Overemphasis of one detail obstructs the view of the whole. Mr. Mörschel need not worry. I shall certainly not cause him to become identified with objections against a religion of which so many of my fellow-men expect contentment in this life and eternal happiness thereafter.

Nevertheless, I must also do justice to his penetrating insight. What he saw was, at least in part, not wrong. It is true that I recognize no eternal verities except those which can not only be comprehended by the human intellect but also be demonstrated and verified by man's reason. It is, however, a misconception of Judaism if Mr. Mörschel thinks I cannot take this position without deviating from the religion of my fathers. On the contrary, I consider this view an essential aspect of the Jewish religion and believe that this teaching represents one of the characteristic differences between Judaism and Christianity. To sum it up in one sentence: I believe Judaism knows nothing of a *revealed religion* in the sense in which Christians define this term. The Israelites possess a *divine legislation*—laws, commandments, statutes, rules of conduct, instruction in God's will and in what they are to do to attain temporal and eternal salvation. Moses, in a miraculous and supernatural way, revealed to them these laws and commandments, but not dogmas, propositions concerning salvation, or self-evident principles of reason. These the Lord reveals to us as well as to all other men at all times through nature and events but never through the spoken or written word.

I am afraid many readers will once again find my views shocking and hard to accept. People have usually paid little attention to this distinction. Supernatural *legislation* has been mistaken for a supernatural *revelation* of religion; and people have spoken of Judaism as if it were merely an earlier revelation of those religious doctrines and tenets which are necessary for man's salvation. Therefore, I shall have to explain my views in some detail in order to avoid further misunderstandings. Let me go back to first principles so that my reader and I can set out and proceed together from the same starting point.

Those principles which are independent of time and remain forever unchanged are called *eternal truths*. They are either *necessary*, and as such, unchangeable, or *contingent;* that is, either their permanence is grounded in their *essence* (they are what they are because logically they cannot be anything else and are not conceivable in any other way), or it is based on their reality (they are universally true because they occurred and became real in this and in no other way, and they could not have achieved reality in any other or better way than they did). In other words necessary as well as contingent truths have a common source—truth. The former originate in reason, the latter in the will of God. The statements of necessary truths are true because God conceives of them this way and not otherwise; the statements of contingent truths are true because God, who in His wisdom has given them, considers them to be good this way and not otherwise. Examples of the first kind are the principles of pure mathematics and logic; examples of the second are the general principles of physics and psychology—the laws of nature according to which this universe, matter as well as spirit, is governed. Necessary truths cannot be changed even by God himself. Even He, notwithstanding His omnipotence, cannot suspend the rules of His unchangeable reason. Contingent truths, however, are subject to the will of God; they are unchangeable only insofar as they are in accord with His holy will and intentions. He can suspend them, permit exceptions [miracles], or introduce different laws in their stead as often as such changes may be useful.

Besides these eternal truths there also exist temporal, historical truths—events which occurred once and may never occur again, or principles which, by the processes of cause and effect, become accepted as truth at a certain point in time and space. They can be considered true only in relationship to this particular point in time and space. All historical truths fall into this category—events which took place long ago and of which we were told by others but which we ourselves can no longer observe.

These categories of truth differ not only in their essential nature but also with regard to the method by which they can be taught, that is, in the way in which men can convince themselves and others of their truth. Necessary truths are based upon reason, i.e., upon the unchangeable logical relationship and essential coherence of concepts, according to which they either presuppose or exclude each other. All mathematical and logical proofs are of this kind. They show whether it is possible or impossible to establish a logical relationship between certain concepts. If we wish to teach these truths to others, we must not appeal to their faith but address ourselves to their reason. We need not quote authorities or refer to the credibility of men who hold the same views but must analyze the components of these concepts and demonstrate their logical connection step by step until our student will understand how they are interrelated. Our function in this educative process, as Socrates put it so well, is merely a kind of midwifery. We cannot put anything into the other's mind that is not already there; we can, however, assist him in his effort to bring to light what was hidden and make him perceive and comprehend what he has so far failed to see.

The apperception of the truths in the second category, however, requires not only reason but also *observation*. If we want to know what laws the Creator has prescribed for His creation or according to what general rules nature changes, we must experience, observe, and analyze individual facts and events. Our first step must be to gather all pertinent data by using the evidence of our senses; the next step must then be to use our reason in order to determine what the different cases may have in common. To be sure, we shall have to accept some conclusions on faith, based on the experience and views of others. Our life span simply is not long enough to allow us to experience everything for ourselves. Hence, in many cases we rely on the findings of reputable scholars, on the assumption that their experiments and observations are correct. But we should rely on them only insofar as we ourselves know or are convinced that the objects of their investigation still exist, that their experiments and observations can be repeated, and that their results can be examined by us or others who have the opportunity or capacity to do so.

Yet if the results of these investigations are of great importance for our own or someone else's happiness, we will rarely be satisfied to rely on the statements even of credible witnesses who tell us of their experiments and observations. In such cases, we will seek an opportunity to repeat the experiments ourselves and let the evidence of our own observations convince us. The Siamese, for instance, may be prepared to trust the reports of the Europeans that in their part of the world water hardens and can carry heavy burdens at certain times. They may accept this finding on faith and perhaps even announce it as a fact in their textbooks of physics, on the premise that is always possible to verify this observation by experiment. Should they, however, find themselves in a situation in which their lives are endangered and in which they might have to entrust themselves or their families to this hardened element, they would hardly feel adequately reassured by a mere report which they have received from someone else. They would want to convince themselves of its truth by their own experiments, tests, and observations.

Historical truths—the passages, so to speak, which occur only once in the book of nature—must, however, be explained by themselves or they will remain incomprehensible. They can have been perceived only by the senses of those who were present at the time and place they occurred in nature. Everyone else must accept them on the authority and testimony of others. Moreover, people who live at a subsequent time must rely unconditionally on the credibility of this testimony, for it testifies to something which no longer exists. The object itself as well as the opportunity for direct observation to which they could appeal can no longer be found in nature, and the senses can no longer convince themselves of the facticity of the object or the truth of the event. Hence, the reputation and credibility of the narrator are the sole evidence in historical matters. Without [the] testimony [of eyewitnesses] we cannot be convinced of any historical truth. Without authority the truth of history vanishes along with the event itself.

Whenever God intends man to understand a certain truth, His wisdom provides man with the means most suited to this purpose. If it is a necessary truth, God provides man with whatever degree of reason he requires for its understanding. If a natural law is to be disclosed to man, God's wisdom will provide him with the necessary capacity for observation; and if a historical truth is to be preserved for posterity, God's wisdom authenticates its historicity by establishing the narrator's credibility beyond any doubt.

It seems to me that only with regard to historical truths did God, in His supreme wisdom, have to instruct mankind either by human means—through the spoken or written word—or through extraordinary events and miracles, if they were required to confirm the authority and credibility of the event. But the eternal truths that are necessary for man's salvation and happiness are taught by God in a manner that is more fitting for His dignity: not through sounds or letters—intelligible only here or there, to one or the other individual—but through creation itself in all its inter-relatedness, which is legible and intelligible to all men. Nor does He confirm these truths by miracles which would merely fortify our belief in the credibility of certain historical events. Instead, He awakens our mind, which He himself has created, and gives it an opportunity to observe the inter-relatedness of things as well as its own workings and to convince itself of those truths which destiny enables man to understand in this life on earth.

Consequently, I do not believe that human reason is incapable of perceiving those eternal truths which are indispensable to man's happiness or that God, therefore, had to reveal these truths in a supernatural way. Those who cling to this notion subtract from God's omnipotence the very thing they think they are adding to it. They assume He was good enough to disclose to men those truths on which their happiness depends, but that He was neither omnipotent nor good enough to grant them the capacity to discover these truths for themselves. Moreover, those who take this position consider the necessity for a supernatural revelation more universal than revelation itself does. If mankind, without revelation, cannot be but corrupt and miserable, why should by far the larger part of mankind have been compelled to live without benefit of true revelation from the beginning? Why should the two Indies have to wait until it should please the Europeans to send them missionaries with a message of comfort without which, according to this opinion, the Indians can live neither virtuously nor happily? Moreover, it is a message which they can neither fully comprehend nor properly utilize because of their limited circumstances and state of knowledge.

According to the tenets of Judaism, all inhabitants of the earth have a claim to salvation, and the means to attain it are as widespread as mankind itself, as liberally dispensed as the means of satisfying one's hunger and other natural needs. [Men can attain salvation regardless of] whether they still live in that crude and primitive state in which nature is not yet conscious of its creative power and is only able to express itself stammeringly, as it were; or whether their culture is highly developed, illumined by the arts and sciences, and man has learned to use words and images to express his inward perceptions and to transform them into intelligible signs and symbols.

As often as it was necessary, Providence made wise men arise in every nation and bestowed upon them the gift to look with a clear eye into themselves as well as around themselves, to contemplate God's works, and to communicate their insights to others. But this is not always necessary or even practical. Often, the babbling of infants and babes will suffice, as the psalmist says, to confound the enemy. The simple, unsophisticated man has not yet discovered the factitious type of argument that tends to confuse the more sophisticated person. For him, the word "nature" is mere sound and has not yet become a force that seeks to supplant the Deity. He knows but little of the difference between mediate and immediate effects. In fact, he hears and sees the all-animating power of the Deity everywhere—in every sunrise, in every rainfall, in every flower that unfolds, in every lamb that grazes in the meadow, glad to be alive. This way of looking at things may be fallacious, but it leads to the immediate recognition of an invisible, all-powerful being to whom we owe all the good which we enjoy. As soon, however, as an Epicurus or a Lucretius, a Helvetius, or a Hume begins to criticize the inadequacies of these notions and, going to the opposite extreme (a weakness which is all too human), begins to play deceptive and bewildering games with the term "nature," Providence produces yet another kind of man, one who is able to separate mere prejudice from truth, to correct the exaggerations of both extremes, and to show that truth will emerge where prejudice is discarded. Basically, however, the human material is everywhere the same, whether it merely uses the crude and robust energy with which nature has endowed it or whether its taste has become so refined by culture and art that, like a person weakened by illness, it finds intellectual food palatable only if it is appetizingly prepared and daintily served.

Man's actions and moral conduct, on the whole, probably benefit just as much from these primitive notions as they do from those refined and purified concepts. Some nations are destined by Providence to go through the full cycle of these notions, occasionally even more than once. Nevertheless, the extent and intensity of their morality remain essentially unchanged throughout the diversity of these successive epochs.

I, for my part, cannot share the view of mankind's education into which my late friend, Lessing,[23] was misled by I don't know what scholar of history. He conceives of mankind not as a collectivity but as an individual whom Providence, as it were, has sent to school here on earth in order to raise him from childhood to manhood. Basically—to use the same metaphor—mankind, in nearly every century, is simultaneously youthful, mature, and old, but in different places and regions of the world. Here it is still in the cradle, breast feeding or living on cream and milk. There it stands in manly posture, consuming the meat of cattle; and in still another place, it is already tottering, leaning on a cane, toothless once again. "Progress" is a term that applies only to the individual, destined by Providence to spend part of his eternity here on earth. Everyone goes through life in his own way. One man's path leads through flowers and meadows; another man's path takes him through arid plains, across steep mountains, or past dangerous abysses. But all of them progress on their journey, as they travel on the road to whatever happiness destiny may have in store for them. That it could, however, also have been the intention of Providence to let mankind as a whole advance steadily and toward perfection in the course of time and here on earth, is something I cannot believe. At least, this is by no means an established fact, nor is it a logically necessary assumption that has to be made to prove the providence of God, as many people like to think.

How strange that we stubbornly tend to reject all theories and hypotheses, prefer to speak of facts and, indeed, want to listen to nothing but facts, yet look for facts least where they matter most. You want to divine what designs Providence may have for mankind? Do not frame hypotheses! Simply look around and observe what actually happened. All this is *fact*—it must be part of the original design [of God] and must have been allowed for or at least included in wisdom's plan. Providence never fails to accomplish its goal. Everything that happens must have been either part of the initial design or at least compatible with it.

If you take mankind as a whole, you will not find that there is constant progress in its development that brings it ever nearer to perfection. On the contrary, we see constant fluctuations; mankind as a whole has never yet taken any step forward without soon and with redoubled speed sliding back to its previous position. Most nations remain on the same level of culture for many centuries, in the same twilight, one which seems much too weak for our pampered eyes. Occasionally a dot in a huge mass will start glowing, become a brilliant star, and traverse its course, which, after a shorter or longer period, sets it down once again in or near the place where it had originated.

Individual man makes progress; but mankind oscillates continually within fixed limits. Seen as a whole, however, mankind has clearly maintained virtually the same degree of morality through all fluctuations and periods—the same mixture of religion and irreligion, of virtue and vice, of happiness and misery. There is that balance of good and evil which is necessary for the individual's education on earth in order to enable him to approach perfection as closely as is commensurate with his gifts and the destiny apportioned to him.

To return now to my previous remarks. Judaism does not claim to possess the exclusive revelation of eternal truths that are indispensable to salvation. It does not claim to be a "revealed religion," as this term is commonly understood. Revealed *reli-*

gion is one thing, revealed *legislation,* another. The voice that was heard at Sinai on that great day did not proclaim, "I am the Eternal, your God, the necessary autonomous Being, omnipotent and omniscient, who rewards men in a future life according to their deeds." This is the universal religion of mankind, not Judaism; and this kind of universal religion—without which man can become neither virtuous nor happy—was not and, in fact, could not have been revealed at Sinai. For who could have needed the sound of thunder and the blast of trumpets to become convinced of the validity of these eternal verities? Surely not the unthinking, animal-like man whom his own reflections had not yet taught to acknowledge the existence of an invisible being that governs the visible world. The miraculous voice could not have instilled any such concept in this kind of person and, consequently, could not have convinced him. Nor could it have affected the sophist whose ears are buzzing with so many doubts and brooding questions that he can no longer hear the voice of common sense. He demands rational proofs, not miracles. And even if the great Master ["Teacher"] of religion were to awaken all the dead from the dust on which they once stood in order to confirm thereby an eternal truth, the skeptic would still say, "The Teacher has revived many dead, yet I still know no more about eternal truth than I did before. All I know now is that someone can do, and make us hear, extraordinary things. But can there not possibly be several such beings that simply do not consider it advisable to reveal themselves at this moment?" How far all this is still removed from the infinitely exalted idea of a unique, eternal deity that rules the entire universe according to its unlimited will and is able to discern men's innermost thoughts in order to reward them according to their merit, if not here then in the hereafter!

Anyone who did not know this, who was not imbued with these truths which are indispensable to man's happiness, and therefore approached the holy mountain unprepared could perhaps be stunned and overwhelmed by the great and miraculous events that took place there, yet he still would not have caught the truth.

No, all this was supposed to be already known; it had probably been taught and explained to the people during the days of preparation. Proved by human reason, it was certain beyond all doubt. And now the divine voice proclaimed, "I am the Lord, your God, who brought you out of the land of Egypt, the house of bondage" [Exod. 20:2]. A historical fact, on which this people's legislation was to be founded, as well as laws were to be revealed here: commandments and ordinances, but no immutable religious truths. "I am the Lord, your God, who made a covenant with your fathers, Abraham, Isaac, and Jacob, and who swore unto them to raise a people from their seed unto Myself. The time for the fulfillment of this promise has finally come. To this end, I have redeemed you from the Egyptian slavery— redeemed you with unheard-of miracles and signs. I am your Redeemer, your Sovereign and King. I now make a covenant with you and give you laws by which you are to live and become a happy people in the land which I shall give you." All these are historical truths which, by their very nature, rest on historical evidence, *must* be verifiable by authority, and *can* be confirmed by miracles.

Miracles and extraordinary signs, according to Judaism, are no proofs for or against the eternal verities [that can be demonstrated by reason]. Therefore, Scripture itself instructs us not to listen to a prophet who teaches or counsels things which are contrary to established truth, even if he were to confirm his message by miracles. Indeed, the man who performs miracles must be condemned to death if he tries to mislead us into idolatry. Miracles can merely verify testimonies, support authority, and strengthen the credibility of witnesses and of those who transmit tradition. But no testimony or authority can invalidate an established truth that is demonstrable by reason or make a doubtful idea less doubtful and uncertain.

Although the Divine Book which we received through Moses is essentially a book of laws, containing ordinances, rules of conduct, and prescriptions, it also includes, as is well known, an inexhaustible treasure of rational truths and religious precepts. They are so inseparably intertwined with the laws as to form an indivisible whole. All laws refer to, or are based upon, eternal verities, or remind us of them, or induce us to ponder them. Hence our rabbis rightfully said that "Laws are related to doctrines as the body is to the soul." I shall have more to say about this later.

Right now, I simply want to state it as a fact which can be verified by anyone who consults the laws of Moses, even if only in a translation. The experience of many centuries also teaches that this divine law book has become the source of knowledge from which a large segment of mankind draws new insights or corrects old notions. The more you search in it, the greater will be your amazement about the depth of the insights hidden in it. To be sure, this book, at first glance, seems to present truth in its simplest attire, as it were—without adornment or pretensions. Yet the more closely you approach the truth and the purer, the more innocent, more loving and longing is the glance with which you look upon it, the more it will unfold its divine beauty, veiled lightly so as not to be profaned by vulgar and unholy eyes.

But all these excellent notions address themselves not to our ability to believe but to our capacity to understand and reflect. Among the precepts and ordinances of the Mosaic law, there is none saying, "You shall believe" or "You shall not believe." All say, "You shall do" or "You shall not do." You are not commanded to believe, for faith accepts no commands; it accepts only what comes to it by reasoned conviction.

All commandments of the divine law are addressed to man's will, to his capacity to act. In fact, the original Hebrew term [*emunah*] that is usually translated as "faith" means, in most cases, merely "trust," confidence, or firm reliance on pledge and promise: "Abraham trusted in the Lord, and He counted it to him for righteousness" [Gen. 15:6]; "And Israel saw . . . and trusted the Lord and Moses, His servant" [Exod. 14:31]. Whenever the text refers to eternal verities, it does not use the term "believe" but "understand" and "know": "Know that the Lord is God, and there is none beside Him" [Deut. 4:35]; "Therefore know this day and take it to heart that the Lord alone is God, in the heavens above and on the earth below, and there is none else" [*ibid.*, 4:39]; "Hear, O Israel, the Lord our God, the Lord is One" [*ibid.*, 6:4]. Nowhere does a passage say, "Believe, O Israel, and you will be blessed; do not doubt, O Israel, lest you will be punished." Commandment and prohibition, reward and punishment apply only to acts of commission and omission. These acts are governed by our ideas of good and evil and hence are affected by our hopes and fears. Beliefs and doubts, however, intellectual assent or dissent are governed neither by our wishes or desires nor by our fears and hopes but by what we perceive to be true or false.

For this reason, Judaism has no symbolic books, no articles of faith. No one has to swear to creedal symbols or subscribe, by solemn oath, to certain articles of faith. We do not require the affirmation of specific doctrines by oath. In fact, we consider this practice incompatible with the true spirit of Judaism. Maimonides[24] was the first thinker to whom it occurred by chance to try to condense the religion of his fathers into a certain number of principles. According to his explanation, he wanted religion, like all other sciences, to have axioms from which everything else could be deduced. This accidental effort produced the Thirteen Articles of Faith, to which we owe the hymn *Yigdal*,[25] as well as some valuable writings by Chasdai, Albo, and Abarbanel. But these are the only results which Maimonides' effort to formulate specific articles of faith has produced. Thank God, they have not been forged into shackles for our beliefs. Chasdai opposes them and proposes certain changes. Albo limits their number and wants to recognize only three basic principles, which correspond more or less to those which Herbert of Cherbury later proposed as basis for a catechism. Still others, especially Luria and his disciples, the neo-Kabbalists, refuse to recognize any fixed number of fundamental tenets and maintain that everything in our teachings is axiomatic.[26] Yet all these controversies were conducted, as all controversies of this kind should be, with earnestness and zeal but without animosity and bitterness. And although Maimonides' Thirteen Articles of Faith have been accepted by the majority of our people, no one, to the best of my knowledge, has ever accused Albo of being a heretic because he attempted to reduce their number and to base them on more universal rational principles. In matters of this kind, we still heed the important dictum of our sages, "Although this one permits and the other prohibits, both teach the words of the living God." [27]

Here, too, everything depends on the basic distinction between believing and knowing, between religious thought and religious act. To be sure, human knowledge can be reduced to a few fundamental concepts which may be considered axiomatic. The fewer these are, the firmer will the superstructure stand. Laws, however, are irreducible. In their case, every detail is essential. Therefore, we are justified in saying that "to us, *all* words of Scripture, all commandments and prohibitions of God are fundamental." Should you, nevertheless, want to know what their quintessence is, listen to how it was defined by one of the great teachers of our people, Hillel the Elder, who lived before the destruction of the Second Temple. Once a heathen said to him, "Rabbi, teach me the entire law while I am standing on one foot." Shammai, whom the man had previously annoyed with the same request, had dismissed him contemptuously. But Hillel, renowned for his imperturbable equanimity and gentleness, replied, "My son, love thy neighbor as thyself. This is the entire law; the rest is commentary. Now go and study." [28]

I have now sketched the basic outlines of ancient Judaism in its pristine form. As I see it, Judaism has from its inception consisted of both doctrines and laws, convictions and actions. The doctrines of Judaism were never tied to phrases or formulations which had to remain unchanged for all men and times, throughout all revolutions of language, morality, ways of life, and circumstances. Written words are fixed forever, immutable. They represent rigid and unchangeable forms into which our concepts cannot be forced without being mutilated. [In Judaism, however,] our doctrines became part of a living tradition which was transmitted through oral instruction. Thus, it could keep pace with all changes of time and circumstances; it could be altered and molded according to the needs and intellectual capacities of each student. Our forefathers felt that their right to teach this oral tradition could be derived from the text of the written law

itself as well as from the ceremonial acts which every adherent of
Judaism is obligated to practice unceasingly.

At first, it was explicitly forbidden to add anything in writing
to the laws which Moses had recorded for the people in accordance with God's instructions. According to our rabbis, you are
not permitted to write down what has been transmitted orally.
It was only much later that the heads of the Synagogue decided,
albeit with considerable reluctance, to grant permission—which
had by then become necessary—to record some legal traditions
in writing. They called this permission "a destruction of the
law," saying with the psalmist, "It is a time when for the sake
of the Lord the law must be destroyed" [Ps. 119:126].[29]

Yet this development was not in harmony with the original
intent. The ceremonial law itself is a living kind of script, as it
were, stirring heart and mind, full of meaning, stimulating man
to continuous contemplation. What a student himself did and saw
being done by others from morning till night pointed to religious
tenets and convictions and spurred him on to emulate his teacher,
to observe him, to take note of his actions, and thus to obtain the
instruction that was commensurate with his capacities and merited by his conduct.

The ready availability of books and other printed materials,
whose number has enormously increased since the invention of
the printing press, has changed man radically. It has revolution-
ized human thought and knowledge. This development has, of
course, been beneficial and contributed to the improvement of
mankind—something for which we cannot be grateful enough
to Providence. But like every good thing that happens to man
on earth, it also has some evil side effects, partly owing to abuse
and partly to the inevitable limitations of the human condition.
We teach and instruct each other through writings; we get to
know nature and men only from writings; we work and relax,
edify and amuse ourselves through writings. The preacher no
longer talks with his congregation—he reads or recites a written
essay; and the teacher reads his written notes from the lectern.
Everything is reduced to the dead letter; the spirit of living
dialogue no longer exists anywhere. We love and vent our anger

in letters, quarrel and become reconciled in letters; our social contacts are maintained by correspondence; and when we do get together, we know of no other entertainment than games and reading aloud.

As a result, a man has lost almost all value in the eyes of his fellowmen. We do not seek personal contact and interchange with a man of wisdom, for we can find his wisdom in his writings. All we do is urge and encourage him to write more if we think he has not yet published enough. Old age has lost its venerability, for the smooth-cheeked youth knows more from books than old age knows from experience. Whether [this knowledge is] fully comprehended or merely half-digested matters little to the youngster. For him, it is enough that he has it, that he carries it on the tip of his tongue, and that he can talk about things more glibly and boldly than the honest old man who probably has all the right ideas but not the right words at his command.

We no longer understand how the prophet could have considered it a terrible wrong for a youth to be overbearing toward an old man. Nor do we understand how a Greek could prophesy the downfall of the state merely because some mischievous youngster had made fun of an old man in a public assembly. We no longer need the man of experience; we only need his writings. In one word: we are *literati*, men of letters [in the literal sense of the word]. Our whole being depends on the printed word, and we can no longer comprehend how mortal man can educate and perfect himself without books.

This was not the case in ancient times. Maybe we cannot say that they were better, but they certainly were different. People drew upon different resources, collected and preserved [knowledge] in different vessels, and transmitted it to the individual by completely different means. Man was more urgently in need of man; theory was more intimately connected with practice, contemplation more closely associated with action. The inexperienced person had to follow in the footsteps of the experienced, the student in those of his teacher; he had to seek his company, observe and sound him out, as it were, if he wanted to satisfy his thirst for knowledge.

In order to show the influence of these factors upon religion and morals more clearly, I must once more permit myself a digression from my path, to which, however, I shall soon return. My material touches upon so many issues that I cannot always keep a straight course and must take an occasional side road.

It seems to me that the change in written symbols which characterizes different cultural periods has played an important role in the revolutionary developments that have taken place in man's knowledge and, especially, in his religious concepts and convictions. While this change was not the sole cause of these developments, it affected them significantly. As soon as man ceases to be satisfied with the first impressions of his senses (and who can long remain satisfied with them?), as soon as his soul begins to distill his external impressions into concepts, he becomes aware of the need to embody these concepts in visible symbols, not only as a means of communication with others but also as an aid to his memory and, if needed, for later recall. Actually, he may be able to (and, indeed, may have to) take the first steps toward abstraction and the formulation of general characteristics without the use of signs and symbols; for all abstract concepts are initially formed without the assistance of symbols and are only later designated by a name.

Our power of observation must first separate the common characteristic from the tissue with which it is interwoven, thus making it distinctive and evident. Two factors are involved in this process: the objective impact of the impression which this distinguishing feature makes upon us and the subjective interest we take in it. But the development and observation of the common characteristic require considerable effort on the part of the soul: it does not take long for the light which attentive observation has focused on a particular point of the object to disappear, and the object is soon lost once again in the shadowy mass of which it is part. The soul is not able to advance much farther if this effort must be sustained for a long time or has to be repeated too often. The soul has begun to particularize but cannot yet think. What is it to do?

A wise Providence has given it a means which it can use at all times. It attaches the abstracted characteristic by a natural or arbitrary thought-association to a symbol which is discernible to the senses and which, whenever it is used, recalls and, at the same time, illuminates this characteristic clearly and cleanly. As is well known, man's languages, consisting of natural and arbitrary signs and symbols, came into being in this manner. Without language there would be very little difference between a man and an irrational animal, for without the aid of symbols, man is barely one step removed from [living merely by] physical sensations.

In the same way in which the first steps toward a rational understanding of things had to be taken, the sciences are now being expanded and enriched by inventions. The formulation of a new scientific term is therefore often of great importance. The first man who used the term "nature" may not have made a great discovery. Nevertheless, his contemporaries were greatly indebted to him; he enabled them to confound the juggler who pretended he could make them see an apparition in the air, and whom they could now tell that his trick was nothing supernatural but merely an *effect of nature*. I grant that they did not yet have a clear notion of the properties of refracted light rays and of the way they can produce an image in the air—how much do we ourselves know about this subject today? We have barely advanced a few steps beyond these people and still know very little about the nature of light and its components. But at least they knew that a particular phenomenon could be deduced from a general law of nature, and they found it no longer necessary to ascribe a separate and independent cause to every act of legerdemain.

The same applies to the more recent discovery that air has a specific weight. Although we cannot yet explain the fact as such, we are at least able to relate the observation that liquid *rises* in a vacuum tube to the general law of gravity, even though at first glance it would seem more likely that its weight should actually press the liquid down. We can make it intelligible that the tendency of matter to sink, which we cannot yet explain, has in this case caused the substance to rise. This, too, is a step forward in our acquisition of knowledge. Consequently, not every new scientific term should be considered merely a meaningless phrase because it cannot be deduced from earlier elementary principles. The term will serve its purpose as long as it denotes the general properties and true extension of things. The term *fuga vacui*, for instance, would not have been objectionable had it not been too general for the observations [on which it was based]. People discovered that there are cases in which nature does *not* rush to fill a vacuum immediately. Therefore the term had to be discarded, not as meaningless but as incorrect. Similarly, terms such as "cohesion of bodies" and "general gravitation" still retain their importance for science, even though we do not yet know how to deduce them from earlier principles.

Before von Haller[30] discovered the law of irritability, many scholars must have observed the same phenomenon as they studied the organic nature of living creatures. But the phenomenon was not sufficiently distinctive from secondary phenomena to hold the attention of the observer after the initial discovery. Whenever the phenomenon recurred, he considered it merely an isolated natural effect; it did not remind him of the numerous cases in which he had previously observed it. Therefore, it quickly disappeared again from attention, as it had done on all previous occasions, without leaving a trace or recollection in his mind. Von Haller alone succeeded in isolating the phenomenon from others. He perceived its general nature and gave it a name. Now that he has brought it to our attention, we know how to relate each particular case in which we discover something similar to a general law of nature.

It is, therefore, doubly necessary to give names to concepts. First, names serve, so to speak, as containers in which concepts can be preserved and kept on hand for future use; second, they are the means by which we communicate with others.

Our ability to use sounds or audible signs for the purpose of communication is quite evidently an advantage. For when we wish to communicate our thoughts to others, the concepts are already present in our soul; whenever needed, we can make them intelligible to others by producing the appropriate sounds denoting these concepts.

But this is not the case as far as we ourselves are concerned. If, at any time, we wish to reawaken abstract concepts in our soul and to recall them to our mind through signs or symbols, these symbols will, of necessity, have to present themselves to us of their own accord. They cannot be spontaneously produced or arbitrarily summoned forth by us. Such an arbitrary evocation would presuppose that we are already conscious and aware of the ideas which we want to recall. Here, visible symbols are more helpful. Being permanent, they need not be re-created over and over again in order to be effective.

Concrete objects probably served as the first visible symbols which mankind used to denote abstract concepts. Since every natural object has its own distinctive character which distinguishes it from all other objects, the impression it makes upon our senses will direct our attention chiefly upon the particular features which distinguish it, and stimulate the appropriate conceptualization and designation. In this way the lion probably became a symbol of courage, the dog, of faithfulness, the peacock, of proud beauty. For the same reason, early physicians used to carry live snakes around to symbolize their claim that they knew how to render the harmful harmless.

As time went by, people probably found it more convenient to carry or use two- or three-dimensional *images* of objects instead of the objects themselves. Later, they began to use mere graphic outlines for the sake of brevity. Still later, merely a part of the outline was used to represent the whole, until finally a shapeless but meaningful whole was fashioned out of heterogeneous parts. This method of notation is called *hieroglyphics*.

This development probably took place quite naturally. But the transition from hieroglyphics to our written alphabet seems to have required a leap, and the leap itself must have required extraordinary human ingenuity.

Some people make the assumption that our written alphabet merely represents a series of sounds and that sounds alone can denote objects and ideas. This assumption is completely without foundation. True, for those of us whose sense of auditory perception is highly developed, writing evokes primarily the *spoken* word. In other words, for us, language is the path that leads from writing to object. But this need not always be the case. For a person who was born deaf, writing denotes objects immediately; and if he were to gain his hearing, written symbols would, at first, probably continue to call forth in him the objects which they represent, and evoke the corresponding sounds only later. I imagine the major difficulty in the transition to our mode of writing was the need to invent a system [of notation], without adequate preparation or motivation, in which a small number of basic symbols and their possible transposition [metathesis] would serve to denote a multitude of ideas.

At first it must have seemed impossible to survey and classify them all and thereby make them comprehensible. Nevertheless, man's ingenuity was not bereft of guidance in this process. People must have had frequent occasions to transform writing into speech and speech into writing and thus to compare audible and visible symbols. As a consequence, they must soon have noticed that certain sounds recur in the spoken language quite frequently, just as certain figurative components recur in different hieroglyphic images, and that different combinations produce a multiplicity of meanings. Ultimately people must have discovered that the number of sounds which man can produce is not as unlimited as is the number of objects which these sounds denote and that the entire range of intelligible sounds can easily be determined and classified. As time went by, the first fumbling attempts at classification were gradually improved, and a corresponding hieroglyphic symbol was assigned to each group [of sounds].

This development, which reflects one of the most marvelous discoveries of the human mind, nevertheless shows how men, even without soaring ingenuity, could gradually be led to conceive of the immeasurable as measurable; how they learned, so to speak, to divide the starry skies into configurations and to assign every star its place, without actually knowing their total number.

I believe auditory symbols made it easier [than written symbols] for man to trace the configurations and to develop the classifications in which the vast body of human concepts and ideas can be organized. From then on, it could no longer have been very difficult to apply the same method to written symbols which could now also be stratified and classified. I would think that people who were born deaf need far greater ingenuity and inventive power [than we do] to take the step from hieroglyphics to alphabetic writing, because it is not readily apparent that written symbols have a comprehensible range and can be divided into classes.

I employ the term "classify" whenever I want to refer to the components of the spoken languages, for even in today's living and highly developed languages, writing is by far not as variegated as speech, and one and the same written character is read and pronounced differently in different combinations or positions. Thus, it seems quite obvious that, as a direct result of our frequent use of writing, our spoken language has become simpler and, indeed, more monotonous and elementary. The spoken language of people who do not possess the skill of writing is much more variegated, and many of its sounds are so indeterminable that it is virtually impossible to reproduce them accurately in writing. Initially it may have been necessary to proceed without making too many distinctions and to denote a number of similar sounds simply by one and the same letter. Gradually, however, people must have learned to make finer distinctions and to denote them by different letters. But that our own alphabet has been derived from some kind of hieroglyphic writing is a fact which can even now still be discovered by looking at the shapes and names of the letters of the Hebrew alphabet[31] (from which, as history shows, all other known ways of writing are derived. It was a Phoenician who taught the art of writing to the Greeks).

These variations of the modes of writing and notation must have had a significant effect on the development and advancement of our concepts and knowledge. In one respect, this was an advantage. Man's observations, experiments, and theories in fields such as astronomy, economics, morality, and religion could now

more easily be reproduced, communicated, and preserved for the
benefit of later generations. They are like the hives in which bees
collect and preserve honey for their own enjoyment and that of
others. However, as always happens in human affairs, what wisdom builds up in one place, folly attempts to tear down in another, usually employing the very same means and tools. Thus,
misunderstanding or misuse transformed what should have been
an instrument for the improvement of man's condition into a
means for its decay and destruction. What had originally been
simple-mindedness and ignorance now became seduction and
error.

To speak of misunderstanding first. The masses had little or
no understanding of the concepts and ideas which were to be
associated with visible symbols. They tended to regard them not
as symbols but as the things themselves. This error could easily
happen as long as people still used the objects themselves or their
images and outlines, instead of signs and symbols. Objects had a
reality of their own, in addition to their function and meaning as
symbols. A coin, for instance, was simultaneously a symbol and a
piece of merchandise which was useful in its own right. The un-
informed person could therefore easily misjudge or fail to recognize its value as currency. Of course, the inscription on the coin
reduced this danger. At least, it did not encourage it as much as
the outlines of images did. For these outlines were composed of
disjunct and heterogeneous parts; they represented shapeless and
meaningless figures which had no prototype in nature and could,
therefore, hardly be taken for writing. But [precisely for this
reason] this strange and enigmatic combination of elements provided superstition with the material for numerous legends and
fables.

Hypocrisy and willful abuse were busy on their part to sup-
ply superstition with fairy tales which it was not imaginative
enough to invent by itself. Anyone who has attained status and
prestige wants not only to retain but to increase them. And no
one who has ever answered a question satisfactorily will want to
admit that he has no ready answer to every question. No non-
sense is ever too nonsensical, no farce too farcical that people

would not resort to them. No fable is too inane that it would not be propounded to the simple-minded—and all this only so that each "Why?" can promptly be answered with a "Because." The words "I do not know" are indescribably bitter to the man who claims and proclaims that he knows virtually everything, especially if his status in life and the dignity of his office seem to demand such all-embracing knowledge. Alas, how many people there must be whose hearts begin to palpitate when they face the risk either of losing stature and respect [by admitting their ignorance] or of betraying the truth [by denying their ignorance]! And how few possess the wisdom of Socrates to answer, "I don't know," even though they know more than their fellowman, in order to protect themselves from later embarrassment and to make the humiliation involved in a public confession of ignorance easier, should it ever become necessary.

Nevertheless, one can easily see how the worship of animals and images, of humans and idols could have originated in these factors and how they may have encouraged the growth of fables and legends. And though I do not suggest that this is the only source from which mythology grew, I believe it contributed substantially to the rise and propagation of this foolishness. My theory should be especially helpful in explaining a remark which Pastor Meiners[32] made somewhere in his writings. He claims to have observed that among the earliest people, that is, among the peoples that had to develop their culture by themselves and did not owe it to the influence of other people, the worship of animals was more prevalent than that of men and that, in fact, nonhuman objects were considered divine and therefore worshiped far more frequently than human beings were. I assume this observation is correct, and while I leave its verification to the philosopher of history, I myself shall try to explain it.

Whenever men want to use certain objects or their images and outlines to symbolize ideas, they can find nothing more convenient or telling than animals to denote moral qualities. My friend Lessing explains the reasons for this phenomenon in his study of the fable, where he examines why Aesop chose animals to be the actors in his apologues. Each animal possesses a definite, distinctive character, and the fable calls our attention to it not only directly but by emphasizing it repeatedly. One animal is quick, the other, sharp-eyed. This one is strong, that one, calm; this one is faithful and obedient to man, that one is full of deceit or is freedom-loving. In fact, even inanimate things can, at least externally, be more clearly distinguished from each other than men can be. At first glance man reveals nothing—or, rather, everything. He possesses all the qualities described before; at least, his nature excludes none of them completely. But no superficial look can ever reveal immediately which of them is more or less dominant. His distinguishing characteristics are not self-evident, and he is therefore the least-suited object in nature to denote moral ideals and qualities.

Even now, the plastic and graphic arts have no better way to depict the character of gods and heroes than to show them accompanied by animate or inanimate figures. A statue of a Minerva is certainly quite different from that of a Juno, yet the difference between the animals accompanying them is far more telling. The poet, too, often resorts to the use of animals when he wants to speak of moral attributes in metaphor and allegory. Lion, tiger, eagle, ox, fox, dog, bear, worm, and dove—all of them can speak, and the meaning is immediately apparent.

For this reason, it is likely that people used similar symbols in their attempts to express and concretize the attributes of the Most Revered One. Since it was necessary to express these utterly abstract notions through symbols which were least ambiguous and most easily perceptible by the senses, people were probably compelled to select images representing animals. We have already noted how something as innocuous as a mere type of script could quickly degenerate in the hands of some men and lead to idolatry. Therefore, it is quite natural that idolatry was originally more animal worship than worship of man. Men could not be used at all to denote divine attributes, and their deification must have come about in an entirely different way. What probably happened was that in some country there was an influx of heroes and conquerors or sages, lawgivers, and prophets who came from some happier region of the world which had been civilized earlier. These people distinguished themselves so greatly through their extraordinary talents and demonstrated such superiority, that they were revered as messengers of the deity or even as the deity himself. It can, of course, easily be seen why this was more likely to happen among people who owed the development of their culture not to themselves but to others, for, as the well-known saying goes, a prophet is seldom regarded highly in his own country. Mr. Meiners' remark would consequently tend to confirm my hypothesis that the need for written symbols was the first cause of idolatry.

In judging the religious notions of an otherwise unknown people, we must be careful, for the same reason, not to regard everything only from our own point of view, lest we define as idolatry what, in effect, is merely writing. Imagine a second Ombya [i.e., a primitive] who, knowing nothing of the mysterious art of writing, would suddenly and without a chance to get used to our ideas find himself transported from his part of the world to one of the most image-free temples of Europe—or, to give the most striking example, to the Temple of Providence. He would find everything bare of pictures and ornaments, except for some black tracings[33] on a white wall, looking as if they had been put there by chance. Yet the entire congregation would look at these tracings with reverence, directing its adoration toward them, hands folded in prayer. Now take Ombya just as quickly and suddenly back to Otahaiti and ask him to report to his curious countrymen on the religious concepts of the Dessau Philantropin.[34] Would they not simultaneously ridicule and pity the absurd superstitions of their fellowmen, who have sunk so low as to worship black tracings on a white wall as divine?

Our own travelers often enough make similar mistakes when they report to us on the religion of distant peoples. They should familiarize themselves thoroughly with the ideas and views of a people before attempting to say with certainty whether its images still possess the character of writing or have already degenerated into idolatry. When Jerusalem's conquerors were sacking the Temple, they discovered the cherubim on the Ark of the Covenant and mistook them for Jewish idols. They looked at everything through the eyes and from the point of view of barbarians. Judging things by their own customs, they mistakenly regarded a symbol of divine Providence and ever-present grace as an image of the deity, as the deity himself, and their discovery filled them with exultation. In the same way, some reader today will still ridicule the wise men of India who thought that the universe is borne by elephants standing on the back of a large turtle that is being upheld by an enormous bear which, in turn, rests on an immense snake. These good people evidently did not consider the question: On what does the immense snake repose?

But read for yourselves the passages in the *Shasta of the Gentoos* describing a symbol of this kind which probably gave rise to this legend. I am quoting from the second part of the *Reports From Bengal and the Empire of Hindustan*, by J. Z. Hollwell, who had studied the holy books of the Gentoos and was able to look at things from a native Brahman's point of view. These are his own words in Section VIII:

> Modu and Kytu (two monsters, strife and rebellion) had been conquered, and now the Eternal appeared out of the invisible, glory surrounding him on all sides.
>
> The Eternal said, "You, Birma (creative power), create and form all things of the new creation with the spirit I breathe into you. And you, Bistnu (sustaining power), protect and sustain the created things and forms, according to my decree. And you, Sieb (destructive power, power of transformation), change the things of the new creation and transform them by means of the power which I shall give you."
>
> Birma, Bistnu, and Sieb heard the words of the Eternal, bowed, and signified their obedience.
>
> Birma immediately swam to the surface of the Johala (the deep sea), and the children [of] Modu and Kytu fled and vanished when he appeared.
>
> When the spirit of Birma had quieted the deep, Bistnu transformed himself into a powerful bear—a symbol of strength among the Gentoos, since the bear is the strongest animal in proportion to its size—descended into Johala's depth, and with his fangs pulled Murto (the earth) up into the light. Then a powerful turtle (a symbol of constancy among the Gentoos) and a

mighty serpent (their symbol of wisdom) sprang spontaneously forth from him. And Bistnu placed the earth on the turtle's back, set Murto on the head of the snake, etc.

All these ideas can also be found in the paintings of the Gentoos, and one can see how easily the use of such symbols and hieroglyphics can lead to errors.

It is well known that idolatry was actually the dominant religion nearly everywhere for several centuries. Images lost their value as symbols. The spirit of truth which they were meant to preserve evaporated, and the empty container that remained behind was transformed into a dangerously poisonous substance. The notions of the deity, lingering on in folk religions, were so distorted by superstition, so corroded by hypocrisy and priestcraft, that one had every reason to doubt whether atheism would not actually have been less harmful to human happiness, whether godlessness, so to speak, would not have been less godless than such a religion.

Men, animals, plants, even the most abominable and despicable things in nature were revered and worshiped as divine or, rather, feared as divine. For the official folk religion of those days had no conception of the deity other than as a terrible being superior in power to us the inhabitants of the earth, easily aroused to anger, and hard to appease. To the shame of the human mind and heart, superstition knew how to combine the most incongruous notions, permitting human sacrifice and animal worship to exist side by side. In the most magnificent temples, constructed and decorated according to every rule of art, one would look around for the deity worshiped there, only to find a disgusting baboon on the altar, to the disgrace of human reason, as Plutarch put it; and to this monster young men and maidens in the flower of their youth were sacrificed! This is how deeply idolatry had degraded human nature. In an emphatic antithesis, the prophet said, "They slaughtered men in order to offer them to the cattle they worshiped" [Hosea 13:2].

Philosophers occasionally ventured to oppose this universal corruption and attempted to purify and enlighten men's thinking through public or secret instruction. They tried to restore to the images their old meaning or to give them a new meaning and thus to breathe, as it were, the soul back into the corpse. But in vain! Their rational explanations had no influence upon the religion of the people. As eager as the uneducated person may seem to be for information, he is dissatisfied to the same degree when it is presented to him in its true simplicity. What he can easily grasp he soon despises or finds boring, and he constantly searches for new, mysterious, and inexplicable things to which he turns his attention with redoubled gratification. He always wants his curiosity to be aroused but never wants it to be satisfied.

Public instruction found, therefore, no listeners among the masses; in fact, it met obstinate resistance on the part of superstition and hypocrisy and received its customary reward: contempt, hatred, and persecution. And the covert institutions and arrangements through which the rights of truth should have been guarded and preserved at least to some degree became corrupted themselves and developed into seedbeds of every conceivable kind of superstition, vice, and abomination.

A certain philosophical school had the bold idea of separating man's abstract concepts from their representation in images or imaginary configurations and expressing them, instead, by symbols that by their very nature could not be mistaken for anything else: namely, by *numbers*. Inasmuch as numbers as such do not represent anything and are completely unrelated to sense impressions, they were supposedly not liable to misinterpretation. One could regard them as arbitrary symbols of concepts or simply consider them unintelligible. At any rate, these people assumed that even the most primitive mind could not possibly mistake a symbol for its object. Hence, they thought that this subtle device would eliminate all danger of abuse. Numbers are meaningless configurations to anyone who does not understand them. But if they do not enlighten him, at least they cannot lead him astray either.

In this way, the great founder of this school of thought persuaded himself of the validity of his approach. However, unreason very soon returned to its old course even in this school. Dissatisfied with what they found so easily intelligible and comprehensible, people began to look for a hidden power in the numbers themselves. They renewed their search for an inexplicable reality in the symbols, with the result that their value as symbols was lost again. People believed, or at least made others believe, that all the mysteries of nature and of the deity were concealed in these numbers, to which they ascribed a miraculous power—a power through which they sought not only to satisfy their curiosity and inquisitiveness but also their vanity, their striving for unattainable things, their impertinence and greed, their avarice and frenzy. In a word, folly had once again thwarted wisdom's plan and destroyed or appropriated for its own use what wisdom had designed for a far better purpose.

And now I am finally at the point at which I can elucidate my hypothesis about the purpose of the ceremonial law in Judaism. Our people's patriarchs—Abraham, Isaac, and Jacob—had remained faithful to the Eternal and tried to preserve pure religious concepts free of all idolatry, for their families and descendants. And now these descendants were chosen by Providence to be a nation of priests, that is, a nation which, through its constitution and institutions, through its laws and conduct, and throughout all changes of life and fortune, was to call wholesome and unadulterated ideas of God and His attributes continuously to the attention of the rest of mankind.

It was a nation which, through its mere existence, as it were, would unceasingly teach, proclaim, preach, and strive to preserve these ideas among the nations. Initially they lived under extreme pressures among barbarians and idolators, and their misery made them nearly as insensitive to the truth as their oppressors had become because of their pride and arrogance. But God liberated them from their slavery by extraordinary miracles. He became the savior, leader, king, lawgiver, and magistrate of the nation which He himself had fashioned, and He designed its entire constitution in accordance with the wise purposes of His providence. Feeble and nearsighted is the eye of man! Who can say, "I have entered God's sanctuary, comprehended all His plans, and am therefore able to determine the degree, goal, and limitations of His purposes"? The humble inquirer is, however, permitted to form conjectures and to draw conclusions from their results, as long as he remains mindful of the fact that he may do nothing but form conjectures.

We have seen how difficult it is to preserve abstract religious concepts by the use of permanent symbols. Images and hieroglyphics lead to superstition and idolatry, while alphabetic script makes man too speculative—it displays and interprets the symbolic meaning of things and their relationship far too superficially, spares us the effort of penetrating and searching the material, and creates too wide a gap between doctrine and life. To correct these defects, the lawgiver [i.e., Moses] gave the *ceremonial laws* to this nation. Man's daily dealings and conduct were to be linked to religious and moral insights. The law, to be sure, did not impel man to contemplation; it merely prescribed his acts, what he was to do or not to do. The great maxim of this constitution seems to have been: Men must be driven to action but merely stimulated to contemplation.

Therefore, each of these prescribed acts, each rite, each ceremony, had its special meaning and profound significance. It was closely linked to the affirmation of religious truth and moral law through speculation, and it provided an incentive for a man in search of truth to reflect about these sacred matters or to seek instruction from men of wisdom. The truths necessary for the happiness of the entire nation as well as its individual members were to be absolutely independent of all imagery. This was the fundamental purpose and aim of the law. Eternal verities were to be associated solely with deeds and practices, and these were to take the place of the symbols without which truth cannot be preserved. Man's actions are transitory; there is nothing permanent or enduring about them which, like hieroglyphic script, could lead to idolatry through misuse or misunderstanding. Moreover, deeds and practices have an advantage over written symbols: they do not isolate man, do not transform him into a solitary creature, poring over books and articles. On the contrary, they stimulate him to develop social contacts, to emulate others, and to seek oral communication and living instruction.

For this reason, there were but a few written laws; and even those were not completely intelligible without oral instruction and tradition. Nevertheless, it was forbidden to add explanations and comments in writing. It was the unwritten laws, the oral tradition, the living instruction from person to person and from mouth to mouth that were to explain, enlarge, limit, or define more clearly what, by wise intent and in wise moderation, had been left undefined in the written law. In everything a youth saw being done, in all acts, public no less than private, at every gate and doorpost, wherever he turned his eyes or ears, he found an incentive to probe, to think, and to follow in the footsteps of an older and wiser man whose smallest acts and practices he could observe with filial attention to every detail. He felt stimulated to emulate his teacher with a child's eagerness to learn, to discover the meaning and intent of these practices, and to obtain the instruction for which his master considered him ready and prepared. In this way, study and life, wisdom and action, intellectual activity and social intercourse were intimately interwoven. At least this was the way it was meant to be, according to the original arrangement and intent of the lawgiver.

But God's ways are unfathomable. Here, too, things deteriorated after a short period. Before long, this luminous cycle had also run its course. Matters were soon back at or near the low point from which they had started, as the events of many past centuries have unhappily shown only too clearly.

Only a few days after that miraculous event in which they received the law, the people had already lapsed into the sinful folly of the Egyptians and demanded the *image of an animal*. At first they probably did not intend to worship it as a deity. The high priest and brother of the lawgiver would not have consented to this, even if his refusal had endangered his life. They spoke merely of a divine being that was to be their leader and take the place of Moses, who, they believed, had abandoned his post. Aaron was unable to resist the people's demand any longer. He molded a calf for them and, in order to hold them to their resolution to worship not this image but the Eternal One alone, he proclaimed that "tomorrow shall be a feast unto the Lord" [Exod. 32:5]. Yet on the feast day itself, an entirely different notion was voiced by the dancing and carousing mob: "This is your God, O Israel, who brought you out of Egypt" [*ibid.*, 32:4]. With this, Israel's fundamental law was violated, and the nation's covenant was dissolved. Reasonable arguments are rarely effective when a mob is excited and chaos reigns; and the harsh measures to which the divine Lawgiver had to resort in order to reestablish obedience among the rebellious rabble, are well-known. Nevertheless, what commands our attention and admiration even here is the way in which God's providence extracted advantages from this unfortunate event and used it for purposes that were in harmony with the divine intent.

I have already mentioned that paganism had a more tolerable concept of the power of the deity than it had of its goodness. The common man looks upon kindness and a forgiving disposition merely as weakness. He is envious of the slightest advantages anyone else may have in terms of power, wealth, beauty, or honor; but he does not envy his superiority in goodness. And how could he, actually [envy someone else's goodness], since it depends largely on him alone to attain that degree of gentleness which he considers enviable? It takes a good deal of thought to make us understand that hatred and revengefulness, envy and cruelty are basically nothing but weakness and purely a product of fear. Fear, combined with an occasional and insecure sense of superiority, is the mother of these barbaric traits. Fear alone makes us cruel and unforgiving. A person who is secure in the knowledge of his superiority finds much greater happiness in being lenient and forgiving.

As soon as we begin to understand this point, we can no longer hesitate to assign to love at least the same significance and preeminence which we assign to power; to trust that the highest Being, to whom we ascribe omnipotence, is equally capable of infinite goodness; and to recognize that the God of might must also be acknowledged as the God of love. But paganism was far removed from such subtleties. Nowhere in their mythology, poems, or other records of early times can we find a trace suggesting that the pagans attributed even the smallest amount of love and mercy for humans to any of their deities. "The people," says

Mr. Meiners, speaking of the wisest Grecian state, "as well as the majority of their greatest leaders and wisest statesmen considered the gods whom they worshiped as beings more powerful than men, but otherwise sharing their needs, passions, weaknesses, and even vices. To the Athenians as well as to the rest of the Greeks, all gods seemed to be so malevolent that they imagined any extraordinary or enduring good fortune would attract the wrath and envy of the gods, who would wreck it by their machinations. Moreover, the Greeks considered their gods to be so irascible that they felt every misfortune had to be regarded as a divine punishment inflicted upon the people, not because of general moral depravity or some grave individual transgression, but because of insignificant, mostly involuntary cases of negligence during certain rites and celebrations." [35] Even Homer himself, that gentle and loving soul, was unable to conceive of the notion that gods forgive out of love and that, without benevolence, they could not be happy in their heavenly abode.

And now let us see with what wisdom the lawgiver of the Israelites used their terrible transgression against the divine majesty to teach mankind an important lesson and to open a source of comfort from which we can still draw spiritual nourishment. Consider the sublime and awe-inspiring setting: the rebellion had been quelled, the sinners had been made to realize their heinous transgression; the people were dismayed; and God's messenger, Moses himself, was profoundly disheartened.

"O Lord," he implored, "do not force us to leave this place as long as Your anger is not allayed. For how could it be known that I and Your people have found favor in Your eyes unless You go with us? Only when You are really with us shall we, I and Your people, be distinguished from every other people on the face of the earth."

God: "I shall also do what you have asked, for you have truly found grace in My eyes, and I have singled you out by name as My favorite."

Moses, encouraged by these comforting words: "I dare to utter a still bolder wish. O Lord, let me behold Your glory."

God: "I will let all My goodness pass before you[36] and shall acquaint you with the name of the Lord, showing you in what manner I am gracious to whomever I will be gracious, and how I am merciful to whom I will be merciful. You shall see My presence from behind, for My face cannot be seen."

Then the presence passed before Moses, and a voice proclaimed, "The Lord (who is, was, and will be) is the everlasting Being, all-powerful, all-merciful, and all-gracious, long-suffering, rich in steadfast kindness; preserving His loving-kindness to the thousandth generation, forgiving iniquity, transgression, and sin, yet permitting nothing to go unpunished" [Exod. 33:15–23; 34:6f.].[37]

Who is so callous that he can read this and remain dry-eyed? Whose heart is so cruel and hardened that he can still hate his brother, still remain unforgiving?

True, the Lord says He will not allow anything to remain unpunished, and it is well known that these words have caused a great deal of misunderstanding and misinterpretation. However, since they are obviously not meant to invalidate what preceded them, they lead us immediately to the sublime idea which our rabbis discovered in them—that this, too, is a manifestation of divine love, namely, that no man should be exempt from retribution for his transgressions.

An esteemed friend, with whom I once discussed religious matters, asked me whether I would not wish to be assured by a direct revelation that I would not be wretched in the hereafter. Both of us agreed that I did not have to fear eternal punishment in hell, for God will not permit any of His creatures to suffer endless misery. No creature deserves to be eternally miserable as punishment for his conduct. My friend and I had no need to debate this issue. Along with many great men of his church, he had long discarded the hypothesis that punishment for sin should be commensurate with God's offended majesty, that is, infinite. The merely half-true concept of *duties toward God* has produced the equally doubtful notion of an *offense against the majesty of God;* and this notion, taken literally, has in turn produced the unacceptable view that hell's punishment is eternal—a theory which led to gross abuse and brought endless misery to no fewer people in this life than it threatened with unhappiness in the life to come. My philosopher friend agreed with me that God created man for his, that is, man's, own happiness, and that He gave him laws for his, that is, man's, happiness. If the least violation of these laws were to be punished in proportion to the majesty of the lawgiver and, consequently, would result in eternal misery, God would [therefore] have given man these laws [not for his happiness but] for his destruction. Without the laws of so infinitely exalted a being, man would never have to become eternally miserable. O, if it were possible for men to be less miserable without divine laws, who could doubt that God would have spared them the fire of His laws, since it must consume them irresistibly?

On the basis of this premise, my friend's question had to be redefined: Would I not want to be assured by a revelation that I would be exempt even from finite misery in the life to come?

My answer was "No!" This kind of misery cannot be anything but a well-deserved chastisement, and in God's paternal household I shall gladly suffer whatever punishment I deserve.

"But what if the All-Merciful were to cancel a person's well-deserved punishment as well?"

He will certainly do so as soon as the punishment is no longer indispensable for man's moral improvement. No act of revelation is needed to convince me of this truth. Whenever I violate God's laws, I commit a moral wrong that makes me unhappy; and God's justice, that is, His all-wise love, attempts to guide me to moral improvement by physical misery. However, as soon as this physical misery, the punishment for my sin, is no longer needed to make me change my attitude, I can even without revelation be as certain that my Father will remit my punishment as I am certain of my own existence.

Vice versa, should the punishment still be needed for my moral improvement, I do in no way wish to be exempt from it. In the kingdom of our paternal Ruler, the transgressor suffers no other punishment than the one he himself would wish to suffer if he could see its effects and judge its consequences in their true light.

"But," responded my friend, "cannot God consider it necessary to let a person suffer as an example for others, and isn't exemption from this kind of exemplary punishment also desirable?"

My reply was "No." In God's kingdom no individual suffers merely for the benefit of others. Yet should this ever happen, the sacrifice for the benefit of others must confer a higher moral worth upon the sufferer himself. Moreover, as far as his inner growth toward perfection is concerned, he himself must consider it important to have produced so much good through his suffering. In this case, however, I would no longer fear such a state of affairs. Nor can I possibly wish to be assured by a revelation that I should never find myself in a situation in which I would have to manifest a generous benevolence which would increase my happiness and that of others.

All I have to fear is sin itself. If I have committed a sin, divine punishment is actually salutary, an effect of His fatherly concern and mercy. As soon as it ceases to be salutary, I can be sure that it will be remitted. Can I possibly wish that my Father withdraw His chastising hand from me before it has achieved what it was meant to? If I ask God to let my transgressions go unpunished, do I really know what I am asking for? Surely, this too, is a manifestation of God's infinite love that He will allow no transgression of man to pass without retribution. Surely,

> Strength belongeth unto God;
> Also unto Thee, O Lord, belongeth mercy;
> For Thou renderest to every man according to his deeds.
> [Ps. 62:12–13]

That it was Moses who first disclosed God's mercy to the people on this important occasion is explicitly stated by the psalmist in another passage, where he quotes the same words from the Books of Moses to which we have referred before:

> He made known His ways unto Moses,
> His doings unto the children of Israel.
> The Lord is full of compassion and gracious,
> Slow to anger, and plenteous in mercy.
> He will not always contend;
> Neither will He keep His anger forever.

> He hath not dealt with us after our sins,
> Nor requited us according to our iniquities.
> For as the Heaven is high above the earth,
> So great is His mercy toward them that fear Him.
> As far as the east is from the west,
> So far hath He removed our transgression from us.
> Like as a father hath compassion upon his children,
> So hath the Lord compassion upon them that fear Him.
> For He knoweth our frame;
> He remembereth that we are dust.
>
> [Ps. 103:7–14][38]

I am now able to summarize my views of the Judaism of the past and to group them together from an all-inclusive point of view. According to its founder, Judaism consisted of, or was to consist of:

(*a*) Religious doctrines and tenets, or eternal truths about God, His rule, and Providence, without which man cannot be enlightened or happy. These were not forced upon our people under a threat of eternal or temporal punishment but addressed to man's reason, for his rational understanding and acknowledgment according to the nature and evidence of eternal truth.

These truths could not have been inspired through direct revelation; indeed, they could not have been made known through *speech* or *writing*, which can be understood only here and now. The supreme Being has revealed them to all rational creatures through concepts and events inscribed on their souls with a script that is legible and intelligible at all times and in all places. This is why our frequently quoted psalmist sings,

> The heavens declare the glory of God,
> And the firmament shows His handiwork;
> Day unto day expresses His greatness;
> Night unto night makes Him known,
> There is no speech, there are no words,
> Their voice is not heard.
> Yet their sway extends over all the earth,
> And their messages to the ends of the world.
> In the heavens, He hath set a tent for the sun.
>
> [Ps. 19:2–5]

The effect of eternal truths is as universal as the beneficial influence of the sun, which spreads light and warmth everywhere as it circles the globe. The same psalmist has emphasized this point still more clearly in another passage:

> From sunrise to sundown
> The name of the Lord is praised.
> [Ps. 113:3]

or, as the prophet says in the name of the Lord,

> From the rising of the sun to its setting,
> My name is great among the nations,
> And in every place offerings are presented unto My name,
> Even pure oblations,
> For My name is great among the nations. . . .
> [Mal. 1:11]

(b) Historical truths, or accounts of the events of former ages, especially of the lives of our patriarchs; their recognition of the true God; their virtuous conduct before God; their transgressions and the paternal chastisement that followed; the covenant God made with them; and His often-repeated promise to transform their descendants, in the days to come, into a nation consecrated to His service. These historical accounts disclose the fundamental purposes of the people's national existence. As historical truths they must, because of their very nature, be accepted on faith. Authority alone can provide evidence of their historicity. Besides, the nation found that these historical accounts were also confirmed by miracles and supported by an authority sufficiently strong to make their faith immune to all doubts and mental reservations.

(c) Laws, precepts, commandments, rules of conduct: they were to be peculiar to this people, and their observance was to bring happiness to the entire nation as well as to its individual members. The lawgiver was God—God not as Creator and Sustainer of the universe, but God as Protector and covenanted Friend of their ancestors; God as Redeemer, Founder and Leader, as King and Sovereign of this nation. He solemnly sanctioned

His laws, enjoining them upon the people and their descendants as unalterable obligations.

These laws were *revealed*, that is, they were made known by God through the spoken and written word. However, only their most essential part was embodied in letters; and even these written laws remain largely incomprehensible without the unwritten commentaries, elucidations, and specific definitions transmitted by oral and vivid instruction. They are unintelligible, or had to become unintelligible in the course of time, since no words or letters can retain their meaning unchanged from one generation to the next.

The ultimate purpose of the written and the unwritten laws prescribing actions as well as rules of life is [the attainment of] public and private salvation. But to a certain degree, they must also be regarded as a kind of script and have significance and meaning as *ceremonial laws*. They guide the seeking mind to divine truths—partly eternal, partly historical—on which the religion of this people was based. The ceremonial law was to be the link between thought and action, between theory and practice. The ceremonial law was meant to stimulate personal relations and social contact between school and teacher, between student and instructor, and it was supposed to encourage competition and emulation. It actually fulfilled all these functions in early times, before our constitution degenerated, and man's folly interfered once again, transforming, through misconception and mismanagement, good into evil, the useful into the harmful.

State and religion in this original constitution were not united but identical, not joined together but one and the same. Man's relation to society and his relation to God converged in one point and could never come into tension. God, the Creator and Keeper of the world, was at the same time the King and Administrator of this nation. He is a unique Being who admits of no division or plurality in the political or metaphysical spheres. Nor does this Sovereign have any wants. He demands nothing of the people except what will serve their own good and promote the state's well-being, just as the state, for its part, could not demand anything that was contrary to the duties toward God or that had not indeed been commanded by God, the nation's Lawgiver and Magistrate. Every civil act, therefore, was invested with sacredness and religious significance, and every act of civic service became, at the same time, a true act of divine worship. The community was a community of God; its concerns were God's; public taxes were an offering to God; and all life down to the lowliest officer of law enforcement stood in the service of God. The Levites, living on public funds, derived their livelihood from God. They were to have no possessions in the land, for God was their possession. Whoever was compelled to wander outside the country's borders, served alien gods [cf. I Sam. 26:19]. But this view, mentioned in several passages of Scripture, cannot be taken literally. Basically, it means merely that he was subject to foreign political laws which, unlike the laws of his own country, were not, at the same time, religious laws.

The same principle applied to criminal offenses. Every offense against the respect for God, the Lawgiver of the nation, was a crime against the [civil] sovereign and, therefore, a political crime. Whoever blasphemed God, committed lese majesty; whoever desecrated the Sabbath willfully, nullified, as far as He was concerned, a fundamental law of civil society, for the institution of the Sabbath day was an essential part of its constitution: "The Sabbath is an eternal covenant between Me and the children of Israel," said the Lord, "a perpetual sign that in six days the Lord [made heaven and earth." Exod. 31:16f.]. Under the terms of this constitution, such crimes could and, indeed, had to be punished not as erroneous opinions, not as unbelief, but as misdeeds, as willful crimes against the state, designed to weaken or destroy the authority of the Lawgiver and thereby to undermine the state itself.

And yet, consider how lenient the punishment for even these capital offenses was, how extraordinarily tolerant of human weakness! According to an unwritten law, no criminal could be sentenced to bodily or capital punishment unless he had been warned by two witnesses who were not suspect of complicity themselves and who had felt obliged to cite the law to him and to warn him of the prescribed punishment. Indeed, bodily or capital punishment could be meted out only after the criminal had indicated in so many words that he understood and was prepared to accept the punishment [prescribed for his crime] and had committed the crime immediately afterward in the presence of the same witnesses. How rare executions must have been under such conditions; and on how many occasions must the judges have been able to avoid the sad duty of condemning to death a fellow creature and fellow image of God! An executed man, in the words of Scripture, is a derogation of God. How long the judges had to deliberate, investigate, and consider every conceivable extenuating factor before they signed a death decree! Indeed, as our rabbis say, any court which is empowered to deal with capital offenses and is concerned for its reputation must see to it that in a period of seventy years no more than one person ever be sentenced to death.[39]

Hence, it is evident that a man must be quite unfamiliar with the Mosaic laws and the constitution of Judaism if he believes that they bestow rights and power upon the church or authorize temporal punishment for unbelief and heterodoxy. The *"Searcher for Light and Right"* as well as Mr. Mörschel are therefore far from the truth when they think I have abrogated Judaism by my arguments against church rights and church power. One truth cannot clash with another truth. What divine law commands, reason, no less divine, cannot abrogate.

Not unbelief, nor false doctrine and error, but criminal offenses against the majesty of the Lawgiver, insolent violations of fundamental laws and the civil constitution were punished. And even this only when the crime was so outrageous that it exceeded all bounds and came close to rebellion; when the criminal, though well aware of the consequences, did not hesitate to commit his crime before the eyes of two fellow citizens who had reminded him of the law and the punishment it threatened. Here the transgressor against religious law becomes a wanton blasphemer of majesty, a criminal against the state. Moreover, as our rabbis have pointed out, with the destruction of the Temple, all bodily and capital punishments and, indeed, even money fines, as far as they are related to offenses against the state, have ceased to be legal.[40]

All this is in perfect consonance with my principles and inexplicable without them. The civil bonds of the nation have been dissolved. Religious offenses are no longer a crime against the state. Our religion, as religion, knows no punishment, no penalty save the one the repentant sinner voluntarily imposes upon himself. Religion knows no coercion, prods us but gently, affects only mind and heart. I would challenge anyone to give a rational explanation of the [just mentioned] statement of our rabbis unless it is based on my principles!

"But why," I hear my readers ask, "why all this wordy rambling merely to tell us something that is well known? The Jewish polity was a hierocracy, an ecclesiastical government, a priestly state, a theocracy, if you will. We are quite aware of the presumptions which such a constitution permits itself."

Not so! All these technical terms throw a false light upon the matter, and this I had to avoid. It seems that all we ever want to do is to classify and to compartmentalize. As long as we know the heading under which a thing is to be classified, we are content, no matter how imperfect our understanding of it may be. Why do you keep looking for the gender of a thing which has no gender, which defies every classification, which cannot be put under the same rubric together with anything else? This constitution existed only once; call it, if you will, by the name of its founder, the *Mosaic constitution*. It has disappeared, and only the Almighty knows among what people and in which century something similar may appear once again.

Just as Plato spoke of an earthly and a heavenly love, one might also speak of earthly and heavenly politics. Take a fickle adventurer, currying favor, the kind of man found on the streets of every metropolis. Talk to him of the Song of Songs, or of the love of primeval innocence in Paradise, as Milton described it. He will think you indulge in dreams or want to demonstrate to him how well you have learned to besiege the heart of a demure damsel with the help of Platonic endearments. A politician will understand you just as little when you speak to him of the simplicity and moral grandeur of our original constitution. The one knows love only as the satisfaction of base lust, just as the other speaks of statecraft only in terms of power, circulation of money, trade, balance of power, and population statistics. Religion is to him merely an instrument which the Lawgiver uses to keep the unruly man in check, while the priest uses it to suck the people dry and devour their very marrow.

I had to remove this improper perspective, in which we habitually view society's true interests, from my reader's field of vision. For this reason, I gave my subject matter no name but tried to present it on the basis of its own characteristics and purposes. If we look at the issue directly, we shall, as the ancient sage said of the sun, behold in true politics a deity where common eyes see merely a stone.

I have said that the Mosaic constitution did not persist long in its original purity. Already by the time of the prophet Samuel, the edifice had developed a crack which continued to widen until the structure fell completely apart. The nation demanded a visible, bodily king for its ruler. Whether the reason was that the priesthood had already begun to abuse and lose the respect it had enjoyed among the people, as Scripture reports about the sons of the high priest [I Sam. 2:12–17], or that the people's eyes were dazzled by the splendor of a neighboring court—whatever the reason, they demanded to have a king, as all other nations did. The prophet, angered, explained to them what it would mean to have a human king who has his own wants that he can satisfy and even expand at his pleasure. He also pointed out how difficult it would be to satisfy a weak mortal whom one has granted the prerogatives belonging only to God [I Sam. 8]. But in vain; the people persisted in their determination, got their wish, and experienced everything against which the prophet had warned them. In this way, the constitution was undermined, the unity of interests destroyed. State and religion were no longer the same, and a collision of duties was no longer impossible. Such a collision must, of course, have occurred only rarely as long as the king himself not only was one of the people but also obeyed the laws of the land.

But now, follow the course of our history through its varying fortunes and changes, through governments good or evil, god-fearing or godless, right down to the sorrowful period in which the founder of the Christian religion prudently counseled, "Render unto Caesar what is Caesar's, and unto God what is God's" [Mark 12:17], a palpable antithesis [setting the stage for] a conflict of duties. The state was under foreign rule, received its orders, as it were, from alien gods, while the indigenous religion persisted and continued to influence civil life at least in part. Here we have claim against claim, demand in conflict with demand. "To whom shall we give, whom shall we obey?" And the reply was "Bear both burdens as well as you can. Serve two masters with patience and resignation. Give to Caesar, but give to God too." To each his own, since the unity of interest had been destroyed.

And even today, no better advice than this can be given to the House of Jacob: Adopt the mores and constitution of the country in which you find yourself, but be steadfast in upholding the religion of your fathers, too. Bear both burdens as well as you can. True, on the one hand, people make it difficult for you to bear the burden of civil life because of the religion to which you remain faithful; and, on the other hand, the climate of our time makes the observance of your religious laws in some respects more burdensome than it need be. Persevere nevertheless; stand fast in the place which Providence has assigned to you; and submit to everything which may happen, as you were told to do by your Lawgiver long ago.

Indeed, I cannot see how those who were born into the household of Jacob can in good conscience exempt themselves from the observance of the law. We are permitted to reflect on the law, to search for its meaning, and occasionally, where the Lawgiver himself provides no reason [for a particular law], to surmise that it must perhaps be understood in terms of a particular time, place, and set of circumstances. Therefore, the law can perhaps also be changed according to the requirements of a particular time, place, and set of circumstances, but only if and when it pleases the supreme Lawgiver to let us recognize His will—to make it known to us just as openly, publicly, and beyond any possibility of doubt and uncertainty, as He did when He gave us the law itself. As long as this has not happened, as long as we can show no such authentic dispensation from the law, no sophistry of ours can free us from the strict obedience we owe to it. Reverence for God must draw a line between speculation and observance, beyond which no conscientious person may go.

Therefore, I repeat my previous assertion: Weak and nearsighted is the eye of man. Who can say, "I have entered God's sanctuary; I have comprehended the system of His intentions; and know how to determine their measure, goals, and limitations"? I may make conjectures but not decide or act in accordance with my conjectures. If I may not have, without authorization by the legislator or magistrate, the audacity in human affairs to contravene the law and to act on the basis of my own surmises and casuistry, how much less may I do this in divine affairs? To be sure, we are exempted today from those laws which were once, of necessity, connected with land ownership and certain civil institutions [in ancient Palestine]. Outside of Judea, without Temple and priesthood, there can be neither sacrifices nor laws of purification nor levies to support the priests, inasmuch as all these depend on our possession of that land. But personal commandments, duties imposed upon every son of Israel, which are unrelated to Temple service and land ownership in Palestine, must, as far as I can see, be strictly observed according to the words of the law until it will please the Most High to set our conscience at rest and to proclaim their abrogation clearly and publicly.

Here it seems obvious that "what God has joined together, man may not tear asunder" [Mark 10:9]. I cannot understand how any one of us, even if he were to convert to the Christian religion, could believe that he would thereby have appeased his conscience and freed himself from the yoke of the law. Jesus of Nazareth was never heard to declare that he had come to release the House of Jacob from the law. Indeed, he explicitly and emphatically said the opposite and, what is more, did the opposite himself [cf. Matt. 5:17ff.]. Jesus of Nazareth himself observed not only the law of Moses but also the ordinances of the rabbis; and whatever in his recorded speeches and actions seems to contradict this fact, actually only appears to do so at first glance.

Carefully analyzed, all he said and did is in complete harmony with Scripture as well as with [rabbinic] tradition. If he came to put an end to the rampant hypocrisy and sanctimoniousness of that time, he would surely not have been the first to exemplify this very same sanctimoniousness by insisting, through personal example, on the observance of a law which had supposedly already been repealed and abrogated. On the contrary, his entire conduct as well as that of his early disciples is obviously guided and illumined by the rabbinic principle that anyone not born into the law need not bind himself to the law, but that anyone born into the law must live and die in accordance with it. If his followers, in later times, thought differently and believed they could exempt those Jews who accepted his teachings from obedience to the law, they certainly acted without his authorization.

And you, my brothers and fellowmen, who are followers of the teachings of Jesus, how can you blame us for doing what the founder of your religion himself has done and sanctioned by his authority? Can you seriously believe that you cannot reciprocate our love as citizens and associate yourselves with us for civic purposes as long as we are outwardly distinguished from you by our ceremonial law, do not eat with you, or do not marry you? As far as we can see, the founder of your religion himself would not have done these things or have permitted us to do them either.

If this should be and remain your true conviction—which one can hardly believe of truly Christian people—if we can be united with you as citizens only on the condition that we deviate from the law which we still consider binding, then we sincerely regret the necessity of declaring that we shall renounce our claim to civil [equality and] union with you. Everything the humanitarian von Dohm has written[41] will in this case have been in vain, and everything will remain in the intolerable condition it is in now or into which your love of humanity may find it appropriate to put it. It is beyond our power to yield in this matter; but it is nevertheless also within our power, if we have integrity, to love you as our brothers and to implore you as brothers to make our burdens as tolerable as you possibly can. Regard us, if not as brothers and fellow citizens, at least as fellowmen and coinhabitants of this country. Show us ways and provide us with means of becoming better fellow residents, and let us enjoy, together with you, the rights of humanity, as far as time and circumstances will permit. We cannot forsake the law in good conscience—and without a conscience of what use would fellow citizens be to you?

[You may ask,] "But how, then, can the prophecy be fulfilled that some day there will be only one shepherd and one flock?"

Dear brothers, you are well-meaning. But do not let yourselves be deceived! To belong to this omnipresent shepherd, it is not necessary for the entire flock to graze on one pasture or to enter and leave the master's house through just one door. It would be neither in accord with the shepherd's wishes nor conducive to the growth of his flock. [Do you wonder why] some people deliberately turn these ideas upside down and purposely try to confuse them? They tell you that a union of religions is the shortest way to that brotherly love and tolerance you kindhearted people so earnestly desire. If all of us share the same faith, then— as some people try to make you believe—we shall no longer hate each other because of our different beliefs and convictions; religious hatred and persecution will be eradicated; the whip will be wrenched from the hand of hypocrisy, and the sword, from that of fanaticism. This, they say, will be the beginning of the happy days of which it is said that "the wolf will dwell with the lamb, the leopard with the kid," etc. [Isa. 11:6].

The gentle souls who propose such a union are ready to get started with the job right away. They want to act as intermediaries in the humanitarian effort to negotiate an agreement among the faiths, bargaining about truths and rights as if they were cheap merchandise. They want to demand, offer, haggle, threaten, implore, surprise, and outwit until the parties have shaken hands and a contract for the promotion of mankind's happiness can be written and signed. And many others, even though they reject such a scheme as chimerical and unfeasible, nevertheless speak of a union of religions as a very desirable state of affairs, and they are full of pity and sorrow for the human family because this pinnacle of happiness is not within man's reach.

But beware, you humanitarians, lest you listen to such notions without the most careful scrutiny! They may be snares laid by fanaticism (one that is currently powerless) in order to entrap freedom of conscience. You know that this enemy of the good appears in many shapes and forms: the lion's rage or the meekness of the lamb, the dove's simplicity or the cunning of the serpent— none of these postures is so alien to him that he could not adopt it, even if he did not [already] possess it, in order to realize his bloodthirsty designs. Since, as a result of your beneficial efforts, he can no longer openly resort to violence, he may possibly put on the mask of meekness in order to deceive you. Outwardly he may feign brotherly love and radiate a spirit of tolerance, while secretly he is already at work forging the chains with which he plans to shackle our reason so that, taking it by surprise, he can cast it back into the cesspool of barbarism from which you had just begun to pull it up.[42]

Don't think this is merely an imaginary fear, a product of hypochondria. A union of faiths, if it were ever to come about, could have only the most disastrous consequences for reason and freedom of conscience. Suppose people were able to reach agreement concerning the doctrinal formulations they want to introduce as basic creed; suppose one could also manage to find symbols to which none of the religious groups now dominant in Europe could object—what would be gained by this? Would it mean that all of you had arrived at the same views about religious truths?

No one who has the slightest insight into human nature can possibly come to this conclusion. This would merely be agreement on words, on a formula. The unifiers of faith would simply be collaborating in pinching off a bit from some concepts here and there, in enlarging the texture of words elsewhere, until they become so vague and loose that any ideas, regardless of their inner differences, can, if necessary, be squeezed in. Everybody would merely be attaching to the same words a different meaning, peculiarly his own. Therefore, do you still want to boast that you have united mankind in faith, that you have brought the flock under the care of its one shepherd? Alas, if the goal of this universal delusion were to be realized, I am afraid man's barely liberated mind would once again be confined behind bars. The shy animal would soon have let itself be captured and put in harness again. Be as undemanding and conciliatory as you may wish, as soon as you link faith to symbol, tie conviction to words, lay down unalterably your articles of faith, the unfortunate wretch who arrives a day later and dares to find fault even with these inoffensive, purified words, will be in terrible trouble. He is a disturber of the peace! Off to the stake with him!

Brothers, if you care for true godliness, let us not pretend that conformity exists where diversity is obviously the plan and goal of Providence. Not one among us thinks and feels exactly like his fellowman. Why, then, should we deceive each other with lies? It is sad enough that we are doing this in our daily relations, in conversations that are of no particular importance. But why also in matters which concern our temporal and eternal welfare, our very destiny? Why should we use masks to make ourselves unrecognizable to each other in the most important concerns of life, when God has given each of us his own distinctive face for some good reason? Would this not mean that we oppose Providence as far as we can; that we try, in fact, to frustrate the very purpose of creation; and that we deliberately act contrary to our own vocation and destiny in this life and the life to come?

Rulers of the earth! If an unimportant coinhabitant may be permitted to lift his voice and to address you: Do not trust your counselors who, in smooth phrases, seek to mislead you into such a harmful course of action. They are either deluded themselves and cannot see the enemy of mankind lurking in the background, or they deliberately try to deceive you. Our most precious possession—the freedom to think—will be lost if you listen to their counsel. For the sake of your happiness as well as ours, remember that *a union of faiths is not tolerance.* It is the very opposite. For the sake of your happiness and ours, do not use your powerful prestige to give the force of law to some eternal truth that is immaterial to civic well-being; do not transform some religious doctrine to which the state should be indifferent into a statute of the land! Concentrate on what men should or should not do; judge them wisely by their actions; and let us retain the freedom of thought and speech with which the Father of all mankind has endowed us as our alienable heritage and immutable right.

Should, however, the link between privilege and personal conviction have become so solidified over the years, that the time has not yet come to abolish it completely without serious damage, try at least to diminish its pernicious influence as much as you can and set wise limits to an obsolete prejudice.[43]

At least prepare the way for your more fortunate descendants to [reach] that height of culture, that universal human tolerance for which reason is still sighing in vain. Reward and punish no doctrine; hold out no allurement or bribe to anyone for the adoption of a particular faith. Let every man who does not disturb the public welfare, who obeys the law, acts righteously toward you and his fellowmen be allowed to speak as he thinks, to pray to God after his own fashion or after the fashion of his fathers, and to seek eternal salvation where he thinks he may find it. Permit no one in your country to search someone else's heart or to judge someone else's thoughts. Let no one usurp a right which the Omniscient has reserved to Himself. If we render unto Caesar what is Caesar's, then let us also render unto God what is God's. Love truth! Love peace!

COVENANTS—
OLD AND NEW

LETTER TO
JOHANN CASPAR LAVATER [44]

Dear Friend,

You have found it advisable to dedicate your translation from the French of Bonnet's *Examination of the Proofs for Christianity* to me and to request me publicly and solemnly to refute this treatise if I felt that its arguments in support of the claims of Christianity were erroneous. Should I, however, find the arguments convincing, you ask me "to do what wisdom, love of truth, and honor require, and what a Socrates would have done had he read the treatise and found it irrefutable," namely, to abandon the religion of my fathers and to embrace the faith advocated by M. Bonnet. For even if I were ever tempted to stoop so low as to place expediency above my sense of truth and probity, my course of action would in this particular case obviously be dictated by all three elements.

I am convinced your motives are pure and reflect nothing but your loving concern for your fellowmen. Indeed, I should not be worthy of anyone's respect if I did not gratefully reciprocate the affection and friendship for me that are evident in your dedicatory inscription. Yet I must confess that your action has shocked me deeply. I should have expected anything but a public challenge from a Lavater.

Since you recall the confidential conversations I had with you and your friends in my home, you cannot have forgotten how

often I attempted to shift the discussion from religious issues to
more neutral and conventional topics and how strongly you and
your friends had to prod me before I would venture to express
my views on these matters [i.e., Mendelssohn's views on Jesus
and Christianity], which touch upon man's deepest convictions.
Unless memory betrays me, I was assured on these occasions that
our conversations would be kept confidential. I would, of course,
rather be mistaken in my recollection than accuse you of a breach
of promise.

Nevertheless, you could easily have foreseen how repugnant
it would be to me to issue a public statement about these matters
after I had carefully tried to avoid discussing them even in the
privacy of my own home and among just a few trusted men, of
whose good will I was certain. The fact that the voice that now
challenges me cannot easily be disregarded or dismissed only adds
to my embarrassment. What could therefore possibly have motivated you to single me out against my will in order to drag me
into the arena of public controversy, which I had hoped never
to enter? Even if you had ascribed my reticence merely to timid-
ity and shyness, should a loving friend not have shown some tolerance and leniency for such personal shortcomings?

My disinclination to enter into religious controversy has,
however, never been the result of fear of folly. My study of the
foundations of my religious faith does not date from yesterday.
Very early in my life I had already become aware of the need to
examine my views and actions. And the principal reason for
which I have spent my leisure time since then in the study of
philosophy and the humanities was precisely that I wanted to prepare myself for this task. I had no other motives. I knew that my
studies could not possibly bring the slightest material advantage
to someone in my situation. I realized there was no promising
career for me in this field. And as for inner rewards? O, my
dear friend! The civic status and position of my coreligionists
are not conducive to the free development of our intellectual capacities. To ponder the true state of our affairs can hardly increase our happiness. Let me refrain from elaborating this point.

Any person who knows our plight and who has a human heart will understand more than I can possibly say here.

If my decision, after all these years of study, had not been entirely in favor of my religion, I would certainly have found it necessary to make my convictions known publicly. I fail to see what could have kept me tied to a religion that is so severe and generally despised had I not, in my heart, been convinced of its truth. Whatever the result of my studies, I would have felt compelled to leave the religion of my fathers had I ever begun to feel that it was not true. And had my heart been captured by another faith, it would have been depravity not to admit to the truth. What could possibly cause me to debase myself [by not admitting it]? There is only one course, as I have already pointed out, that wisdom, love of truth, and honesty can choose.

If I were indifferent to both religions or mocked and scorned all revelations, I might indeed follow the counsel which expediency dictates while conscience remains silent. What could deter me? Fear of my fellow Jews? They lack the power to intimidate me. Stubbornness? Inertia? Blind adherence to familiar customs and conventions? Since I have devoted a large part of my life to the examination of my tradition, I hope no one will expect me to sacrifice the fruits of my studies to such personal failings.

You can, therefore, see that I would have been impelled to make a public statement about the results of my studies had they left me without the sincere conviction of the validity of my faith. However, inasmuch as my investigations strengthened me in the faith of my fathers, I was able to continue in it quietly, without feeling that I had to render an account to the world of my convictions.

I do not deny that I see certain human excesses and abuses that tarnish the beauty of my religion. But is there any friend of truth who can claim that his religion is completely free of man-made accretions and corruptions? All of us know that the search for truth can be impeded by the poisonous breath of hypocrisy and superstition. We wish we could dispel both without damaging the beauty and truth of the essentials of our religion. Nevertheless, of the validity of the essentials of my faith I am as firmly and irrefutably convinced as you or M. Bonnet is of his, and I declare before God, who has created and sustained both you and me—the God in whose name you have challenged me—that I shall adhere to my principles as long as my soul remains unchanged.

My inner remoteness from your religion has remained unchanged since I disclosed my views to you and your friends [in our earlier conversations]. And I would even now be prepared to concede that my respect for the moral stature of its founder has not diminished since then, were it not that you have clearly disregarded the reservation which I had attached to my views at that time. But there comes a moment in a man's life when he has to make up his mind about certain issues in order to be able to go on from there. This happened to me several years ago with regard to religion. I have read; I have compared; I have reflected; and I have made up my mind [about my religion].

Still, I admit that I would never have entered into a dispute about Judaism, even if it had been polemically attacked or triumphantly held up to scorn in academic textbooks. There would have been no counterargument from me even against the most ridiculous notion which anyone, whether trained or merely semiliterate in the field of rabbinics, might have discovered in some literary trash that no serious-minded Jew bothers to read. I wanted to refute the world's derogatory opinion of the Jew by righteous living, not by pamphleteering. However, it is not only my station in life but also my religion and my philosophy that furnish me with the most cogent reasons why I wanted to avoid religious controversy and discuss, in my publications, only those religious verities which are of equal importance to all religions.

According to the principles of my religion, I am not expected to try to convert anyone not born into my faith. Even though many people think that the zeal for proselytizing originated in Judaism, it is, in fact, completely alien to it. Our rabbis hold unanimously that the written as well as the oral laws that constitute our revealed religion are binding only for our own people. "*Moses* had given *us* the law; it is the inheritance of the House of *Jacob*" [Deut. 33:4].[45] All other nations were enjoined by God to observe the law of nature and the religion of the patriarchs.[46] All who live in accordance with this religion of nature and of reason are called "the righteous among other nations";[47] they too are entitled to eternal bliss.[48] Far from being obsessed by any desire to proselytize, our rabbis require us to discourage as forcefully as we can anyone who asks to be converted. We are to ask him to consider the heavy burden he would have to shoulder needlessly by taking this step. We are to point out that, in his present state, he is obligated to fulfill only the Noachide laws in order to be saved but that upon his conversion he will have to observe strictly all the laws of his new faith or expect the punishment which God metes out to the lawbreaker. Finally, we are to paint a faithful picture of the misery and destitution of our people and of the contempt in which they are held, in order to keep him from a hasty decision he may later regret.[49]

As you see, the religion of my fathers does not ask to be propagated. We are not to send missionaries to the two Indies or to Greenland in order to preach our faith to distant nations. . . . Anyone not born into our community need not observe its laws. The fact that we consider their observance incumbent upon us alone cannot possibly offend our neighbors. Do they think our views are absurd? No need to quarrel about it. We act in accordance with our convictions and do not mind if others question the validity of our laws, which, as we ourselves emphasize, are not binding on them. Whether they are acting fairly, peaceably, and charitably when they mock our laws and traditions is, of course, something else that must be left to their own consciences. As long as we do not want to convince or convert others, we have no quarrel with them.

If a Confucius or a Solon were to live among our contemporaries, I could, according to my religion, love and admire the great man without succumbing to the ridiculous desire to convert him. Convert a Confucius or a Solon? What for? Since he is not a member of the household of Jacob, our religious laws do not apply to him. And as far as the general principles of religion are concerned, we should have little trouble agreeing on them. Do I think he can be saved? It seems to me that anyone who leads men to virtue in this life cannot be damned in the next. (Fortunately, I need not fear that I shall have to defend my views before an academic board of inquiry in the same way in which Marmontel was summoned by the Sorbonne to a hearing because of the convictions he held.)[50]

It is my good fortune to count among my friends many an excellent man who is not of my faith. We love each other sincerely, although both of us suspect or assume that we differ in matters of faith. I enjoy the pleasure of his company and feel enriched by it. But at no time has my heart whispered to me, "What a pity that this beautiful soul should be lost. . . ." Only that man will be troubled by such regrets who believes that there is no salvation outside his church.

Every man, admittedly, has a duty to teach his fellowmen understanding and virtue and to seek to eradicate prejudice and error in every possible way. Consequently, one could assume that a man has the responsibility of taking a public stand against religious notions that he considers erroneous. Nevertheless, not every prejudice or weakness we seem to detect in our fellowmen is equally harmful. Nor should we react to all of them in the same manner. Some prejudices strike directly at the happiness of mankind. Their influence on morality is pernicious; we cannot expect even an incidental benefit from them. These prejudices must be attacked immediately and unhesitatingly by anyone who has the interests of mankind at heart. Any delay or detour would be irresponsible. Fanaticism, hatred of one's fellowmen and the wish to persecute them, levity, self-indulgence, amoral atheism—these are among the failings that disturb man's inner peace and happiness and destroy his latent capacity for truth and goodness before it can unfold.

But some of my fellowmen hold views and convictions which, although I may consider them wrong, do belong to a higher order of theoretical principles. They are not harmful, because they have little or no relationship to the practical concerns of daily life. Yet they frequently constitute the foundation on which people have erected their systems of morality and social order and are therefore of great importance to them. To question such notions publicly merely because we consider them biased or erroneous would be like removing the foundation stones of a building in order to examine the soundness of its structure. Any person who is interested more in man's welfare than in his own fame will refrain from public statements in such matters. He will proceed with the utmost care in order not to destroy someone else's ethical principles, even though he may suspect they are faulty, until the other person is prepared to accept the truth in their stead.

Therefore, I find it possible to remain silent despite the fact that I may encounter racial prejudices and religious errors among my fellow citizens, as long as their views do not subvert natural religion or undermine natural law. In fact, these views may incidentally even produce some good. I admit that our actions do not deserve to be called moral if they are grounded in error and that the cause of the good will be advanced more effectively and lastingly by truth, where truth is known, than by prejudice and error. Nevertheless, as long as truth is not yet known or not yet sufficiently accepted to have the same impact upon the masses that their old prejudices did, their preconceived notions must be considered inviolate by any friend of true virtue.

We must show this kind of discretion especially where a people, though harboring seemingly erroneous beliefs, has otherwise distinguished itself intellectually and morally and has produced a number of great personalities who rank high among the benefactors of mankind. We should, with respectful silence, overlook the errors of so noble a member of the human family even if we think it is all too human on occasion. Is there really anyone among us who is entitled to ignore the excellent qualities of such a people and to criticize it for a single weakness he may have discovered?

These are the reasons, rooted in my religious and philosophical convictions, for which I carefully avoid religious controversy. If you add to them the circumstances of my life among my fellowmen, I am sure you will find my position justified. I am a member of an oppressed people which must appeal to the benevolence of the government for protection and shelter—which are not always granted, and never without limitations. Content to be tolerated and protected, my fellow Jews willingly forgo liberties granted to every other human being. Barred even from temporary residence in many countries, they consider it no small favor when a nation admits them under tolerable conditions. As you know, your circumcised friend may not even visit you in Zurich, because of the laws of your own home town. Thus, my coreligionists owe much grateful appreciation to any government that shows them humanitarian consideration and permits them, without interference, to worship the Almighty in the ways of their fathers. They enjoy a fair amount of freedom in the country in which I live. Should they therefore attack their protectors on an issue to which men of virtue are particularly sensitive? Or would it not be more fitting if they abstained from religious disputes with the dominant creed?

These considerations governed my actions and motivated my decision to stay away from religious controversies unless exceptional circumstances were to force me to change my mind. To the private challenges of some men whom I respect highly I was bold enough to react with silence, while for the little minds that think they can bait me publicly because of my religion, I have nothing but contempt. But when a Lavater solemnly calls upon me, I have no choice but to express my convictions in public, lest my silence be misconstrued as contemptuous disregard or acquiescence.

I have read your translation of Bonnet's essay with close attention. After everything I have already said, I hope there can no longer be any doubt as to whether I found his arguments convincing. In addition, however, I must confess that I do not consider his reasoning even adequate as a defense of the Christian religion, as you seem to do.

Judging him by his other works, I consider M. Bonnet an excellent author. But I have read many vindications of Christianity by our fellow Germans, if not by Englishmen, that are far more thorough and philosophically more acceptable than M. Bonnet's essay, which you have recommended for my conversion. Unless I am mistaken, most of the writer's philosophical hypotheses are of German origin, and even the author of the *Essai de psycho-*

logie,[51] whose arguments M. Bonnet follows so faithfully, owes nearly all his views to German scholars. Where philosophical principles are concerned, a German rarely has need to borrow from his neighbor.

Nor are the general reflections with which M. Bonnet prefaces his work very profound. In fact, I could hardly recognize Bonnet from the illegitimate and arbitrary manner in which he uses this section of his work as an apologia for his religion. I regret that my opinion is so much at variance with yours in this respect; but I have the impression that M. Bonnet's personal convictions and laudable religious zeal led him to ascribe to his truths a cogency that no one else can see in them. Most of his conclusions do not follow from his premises; moreover, I would venture to defend any religion whatever with the identical arguments. This may not even be the author's fault. He evidently wrote only for people who already share his convictions and who read such treatises simply in order to be confirmed in their beliefs. When an author and his reading public hold identical preconceived notions about an issue under discussion, they will readily agree upon its truth.

What amazes me, however, is that you, Sir, consider this study of sufficient caliber to convert a man whose principles must be diametrically opposed to it. It was probably impossible for you to project yourself into the mind of someone for whom these views are not foregone conclusions, but who must first be persuaded of their validity. If you attempted to do this, yet still believe, as you say you do, that Socrates himself should have found M. Bonnet's proofs irrefutable, it can only mean that one of us must be a remarkable example of the influence which prejudice and upbringing exert even upon those who search for the truth with all their heart.

I have given you the reasons for which I fervently wish to have nothing to do with religious disputes. But I have also intimated to you that I could easily present strong arguments in refutation of M. Bonnet's thesis. If you insist, I shall have to overcome my reservations and publish my arguments against M. Bonnet's apologia in the form of a "Counterinquiry." I hope you will spare me this disagreeable task and permit me to return to the peaceful stance which is so much more natural to me. I am sure you will respect my preference if you put yourself in my place and look at the situation from my point of view, not yours. I should not like to be tempted to go beyond the limits that I have set for myself after mature consideration.

I am, with sincerest respect,

your obedient servant,
M. M.

Berlin, December 12, 1769.

ON JUDAISM
AND CHRISTIANITY

First question: On what grounds would a world-renowned philosopher who adheres to the Mosaic law accept the historical validity of the Old Testament, yet reject that of the New Testament?

Your Highness,[52] I cannot trust any testimony which, in my judgment, contradicts an established and irrefutable truth. According to the New Testament (at least as it is expounded in the official textbooks), I must, at the risk of losing my eternal salvation, believe in (*a*) the trinity of the divine Being; (*b*) the incarnation of the Deity; (*c*) the suffering [passion] of one person of the Deity who has divested himself of his divine majesty; (*d*) the satisfaction and gratification of the first person of the Deity through the suffering and death of the second person thus reduced to human status—as well as numerous other similar or subsequent doctrines.

Now, I neither can nor wish to set up my personal views as a guideline for anyone else's thinking. Who am I to be that presumptuous? I myself, however, can accept as truth only what is rationally convincing to me. And I must confess that the doctrines I have just listed strike me as an outright contradiction of the fundamental principles of reason. I simply cannot harmonize them with anything that reason and cogitation have taught me about the nature and attributes of the Deity. Therefore I must reject them. Of course, if I were to find such doctrines in the Old Testament, I would have to reject the Old Testament, too. And even if a miracle worker, in order to verify and validate these teachings, were to revive before my very eyes all the dead who have been buried for centuries, I would still say, "This miracle worker did indeed waken the dead—yet his teachings I cannot accept."

In the Old Testament, however, I find nothing that resembles these doctrines nor anything that I consider incompatible with reason. Therefore, I feel I am wholly justified in having faith in the historic authenticity that we unanimously ascribe to these writings. Consequently, I make the following fundamental distinction between the books of the Old and the New Testaments: the former are in harmony with my philosophical views, or at least do not contradict them, while the latter demand a faith I cannot profess.

I know that some eminent men, who cherish truth as well as Christianity, claim in their private teachings that all these doctrines which seem to offend reason are in reality merely human accretions. According to their theory, which has already begun to receive public attention in England, the founder of the Christian religion was a man just like the rest of us—but also an emissary and prophet of God, similar or even superior to the founder of the Jewish religion. He had been called by God directly to restore the ancient natural religion to its rightful and sacred place, to instruct men in their duties and the road to salvation, and to confirm his teachings by performing supernatural acts. . . .

I would address the following demands to these reformers of the dominant religion:

(a) Unlike M. Bonnet, they must not base their systems on the assumption that Judaism and, to an even larger extent, natural religion are inadequate paths to salvation. Inasmuch as *all* men must have been destined by their Creator to attain salvation, no particular religion can be exclusively true. I dare to assert that this principle is the fundamental criterion of truth in all religious matters. A revelation that claims to be the one and only road to salvation cannot be true, for it is not in harmony with the intent of the all-merciful Creator.

Indeed, a claim to exclusiveness cannot even be justified by the revisions of religion which these teachers themselves suggest. If the founder of this religious movement had merely intended or undertaken to restore natural religion to its rightful place and to assure men of their eternal salvation, it must be possible for me to attain salvation simply by living in accordance with the principles of natural religion and by my wholehearted affirmation of my faith in the immortality of man's soul. The belief that a certain human teacher once had the divine mission of corroborating this doctrine by performing miracles cannot be a necessary precondition for my salvation.

(*b*) I hope this "purified" system of religion will have no room for the doctrine of everlasting punishment in hell. I should also like to see a reform of the doctrine that divine justice demands compensatory satisfaction. Divine justice does not demand satisfaction but punishment—chastisement designed for the sinner's own good. In the divine economy the sinner's penalty is remitted as soon as it is no longer necessary for his welfare.

(*c*) In my opinion, the all-just Being cannot permit that in His kingdom an innocent man should bear the burden of someone else's guilt, even if he were to do it voluntarily. . . .

(*d*) Neither reason nor the Old Testament knows anything about the doctrine of *original sin*. Adam sinned and died. His children sin and die. But it is not because of Adam's fall that they have turned from the good and succumbed to Satan's influence.

(*e*) I should also like to be at liberty to believe of Satan and of evil spirits, only what I consider compatible with reason. The Old Testament says no more about this subject than what can be explained rationally.

(*f*) The founder of the Christian religion never stated explicitly that he wanted to abolish the Mosaic law or exempt the Jews from it. I have not discovered any such statement in the Gospels. In fact, the apostles and disciples were in doubt until much later as to whether pagans who were converted [to Chris-

tianity] would not also have to accept the Mosaic law and be circumcised. It was finally decided not to put too great a burden
upon the pagans. . . .

But I cannot find in the New Testament any grounds permitting the dispensation of Jews from the Mosaic law, even if
they embrace Christianity. In fact, the Apostle himself circumcised Timothy. Therefore, I hope people will concede me the
right to say that, for myself, I see no possibility of exemption
from the Mosaic law.

If, in addition to the modifications of the primary tenets of
religion, the changes [I have just outlined] as well as their corol-
laries were to be accepted and if the New Testament were to be
interpreted and explained accordingly, one would arrive at a religion which could be acknowledged by Christians and Jews
alike. Should this ever happen, the adherents of Judaism, on the
one hand, could well agree that a prophet and emissary of God
once had the mission not to abolish the Mosaic law but to preach
to a corrupted mankind the sacred doctrines of virtue and of its
reward in the life to come. The followers of Jesus, on the other
hand, would have to be concerned only with the affirmation of
those doctrines whose dissemination had been their founder's
mission. If people wish to acknowledge the divine origin of this
mission, so much the better; but it is irrelevant to the truth of
this religion whether people acknowledge, doubt, or even deny its
divine origin.

I cannot repeat it often enough: what matters is the logical
truth of a doctrine, not the historical truth of the mission.

SECOND QUESTION: For what reason do you reject the proofs
for the Christian faith that appear in the Old Testament and are
accepted as divine inspiration even according to the laws of
Moses?

I have read the Old Testament passages on which the truth of
that faith is allegedly based. I have read them repeatedly, with
close attention, and within their context. How unspeakably piti-
able would man's fate be if mankind's salvation were to depend
on this or that particular interpretation of some obscure passage
in a book that had been written in times immemorial for one par-

ticular people in Asia, in a strange and by now dead language! I believe I understand the language of the original text as well as any modern man does. It is, so to speak, my second mother tongue. It seems to me that these passages contain not even the faintest trace of a proof. I do not think I am blinded by prejudice in saying this. In many cases the interpretations of these passages by certain theologians appear to me wrong. In other cases they are highly contrived and arbitrary. To my relief I find that some of the more recent exegetes who approach biblical interpretation with good taste and sophistication have already abandoned many passages once considered fully conclusive. I, for my part, am taking the liberty to consider the disputes about some of these passages merely as an academic game with which I, too, occasionally amuse myself. But . . . I cannot possibly construe Daniel's mysterious dreams as a source containing the key to my eternal salvation, nor can I infer such a thing from some prophet's lofty poetry. These writings are meant to awaken the heart, not to instruct the mind. . . .

Our common Father, who judges us according to our conscience, cannot reject any heart that fervently loves Him, should it go astray because of ignorance and not because of ill will.

> From a letter to Karl-Wilhelm, Hereditary
> Prince of Braunschweig-Wolfenbüttel.

ON REVELATION

As people gradually become more civilized and enlightened, reasoned judgments take the place of previous prejudices [and preconceived notions]. The atheist who demolishes a prejudice that undergirds some practical truth commits an unworthy act. Nevertheless, even such an unworthy act often makes it possible to replace the hollow and crumbling pillars of superstition with more enduring supports. And once the degree of a people's enlightenment permits it, all truths that are indispensable to mankind's salvation can be based upon rational insights.

Is revelation then unnecessary? Yes—for all peoples that did not receive any. The supreme Being would certainly have revealed Himself to them if they were unable to realize the purpose of their existence without revelation. He gave a revelation to the Israelites not because human beings, as such, could not be saved without a revelation, but because it was His wise intent to bestow some particular grace upon this particular people. According to the teachings of Judaism, all other peoples on earth can and ought to live by their natural insights and thus attain salvation. However, the Creator considered it wise, for quite specific reasons, to reveal to this particular people alone special laws by which they are to live and to be governed and by which they are meant to attain salvation.

Since then, it is true, this people has no longer been permitted to seek its salvation on any path other than that prescribed by God. Since then, this people must bear any disgrace, oppression, derision, and persecution it encounters on this path, with patience, in submission to the divine will, and without sidestepping an inch. But no one not born under the Mosaic law is obligated to shoulder this burden. Anyone upon whom God has not imposed these difficult obligations should live according to the law of nature, assured that man, qua man, is innately capable of attaining salvation through righteous living.

The Jew does not claim to be the only creature singled out by God for salvation. What he does claim is that he is the only one who can attain salvation in no other way. He also feels, of course, that he may expect a special reward for his obedience in fulfilling the divine command. Else God would not have granted him this special revelation. One could be perfectly satisfied if the Nazarenes, on their part, were to claim that God had revealed to them, too, the doctrine of immortality by a special act of grace and in an extraordinary way. They are going too far, however, when they consider this revelation as absolutely indispensable and thus deny that God's concern and dominion extend to all peoples. Salvation is the goal of our existence. If God had given the exclusive means for its attainment only to one people—what then should we think of His reign?

From Bonnet's Palingenesis:
A Counterinquiry.[53]

ON MIRACLES

INSOFAR AS every revelation presupposes a historical fact, the truth of that revelation can be substantiated in no other way than by tradition, testimonies, and monuments. But you, Sir, together with other apologists for Christianity, consider miracles to be an infallible criterion of truth. You believe there can be no doubt of the divinity of a prophet's mission if there is evidence that he has performed miracles. And then you proceed to prove —in fact, by very sound logic—that miraculous events are not impossible by definition and that testimonies [verifying their occurrence] can indeed be credible. I referred to this argument when I said that with it one can defend any religion one pleases. Don't you know, Sir, that we—I am referring to my coreligionists —also possess accounts of unprecedented miracles performed by extraordinary men of our faith long after the time of Jesus of Nazareth? Obviously, these accounts are as credible and as venerable to us as yours are to you. Hence we simply have testimony versus testimony! . . .

Would I attempt to defend the religion of Mohammed or that of Confucius with this kind of argument? I do not know whether Confucius claimed that he performed miracles; and his moral teachings do not need my defense. But if Mohammed "condescended," as he himself put it, to perform miracles, and if the Moslems perpetuated the evidence of these miracles by tradition and monuments—how can we refute them? Were we to cast

130

suspicion on the facticity of their primary evidence or on the tradition by which it is perpetuated, they could respond in kind. It is difficult, immensely difficult, to maintain one's own impartiality in such matters. How then can we expect others to accept our judgment when we ourselves are partisans?

The miracles of Christians, Jews, and Moslems contradict each other. Moreover, within each religion itself differing sects proclaim the existence of miracles that are at variance. Where, then, are the criteria by which we can distinguish between truth and error in so crucial a matter?

I, for my part, do not think that miracles were, in biblical times, considered to be infallible evidence of a prophet's divine mission. False prophets were able to perform miracles too—whether by magic, occult powers, or perhaps an abuse of the extraordinary talents given to them for better use, I do not dare decide. The point is that the ability to perform miracles was never accepted as infallible evidence of truth. The lawgiver of the Jews expresses himself unequivocally in this matter [Deut. 13:2–4], and the Nazarene himself speaks just as explicitly and perhaps even more emphatically of the unreliability of miracles: "For there shall arise false Christs, and false prophets, and shall show great signs and wonders" [Matt. 24:24]. Inasmuch as these two lawgivers teach that false prophets, too, can perform miracles, I do not understand how their successors and defenders, contrary to the unequivocal text of Scripture, can claim that miracles are an infallible source of tradition.

The Mosaic legislation presents a different case. It is an event that is not vouched for solely by miracles. For I repeat: Miracles are delusions and were termed "delusions" by Moses himself. His mission rests on a much more secure foundation. The entire people to whom the message was directed beheld the divine manifestation with their own eyes, heard with their own ears that God had appointed Moses as His messenger and herald. Therefore, all Israelites were eye- and ear-witnesses when the prophet received his sublime commission and required no further evidence or proof. This is why it is written, "And the Lord said unto Moses, 'Lo, I come unto thee in a thick cloud, that the people may hear when I speak with thee and believe thee forever'" [Exod.

19:9] and, in another passage, "and this shall be a token unto thee that I have sent thee: when thou hast brought forth the people out of Egypt, ye shall serve God upon this mountain" [*ibid.*, 3:12].

The fact that the law was given publicly was the strongest proof of Moses' mission. It stilled all the doubts and uncertainty that miracles cannot allay. True, Moses performed great miracles. However, once the law had been given, he no longer performed them as proof of his mission's authenticity but only as circumstances and the nation's needs demanded them. And he always referred to God's self-disclosure rather than to his own wondrous deeds when he wanted to chastise the nation for its unfaithfulness.

It is true, of course, that the Israelites were told by God through Moses to obey a prophet who performed miracles while he proclaimed God's commandments to them. However, this is merely a positive commandment according to our religious laws, similar to the law which decrees that a legal decision must be based upon the testimony of two witnesses. The testimony of two witnesses is not absolutely conclusive. Nor is the evidence deduced from miracles. In such cases the positive commandment serves to limit our doubts. It provides us with a definite criterion which is determined by law and thus not subject to the arbitrary interpretation of every individual.

According to the teachings of our religion, any belief in miracles must itself be founded on law and not on subjective conviction. Anyone referring to miracles must take as his basis the law authorizing this belief. But when someone attempts to impose upon us, by logic, the belief that miracles are a conclusive evidence of truth or when someone, out of an unlimited trust in the infallible proof of miracles, wishes to annul our law and to replace it with a new one, we shall be justified in falling back upon our disbelief. We then compare the miracles of which numerous religions boast, contrast each with the other, and deny all of them our approval.

From a letter to Charles Bonnet,
February 9, 1770.

ON MAKING PROSELYTES

I WILLINGLY AND wholeheartedly subscribe to your positive statements about the New Testament's ethical teachings. I gladly believe that Jesus did not teach much of what those Christian teachers preached in his name who, throughout the centuries, persecuted others and, in turn, were persecuted in his name.

A Christianity like yours, Sir, if it were generally accepted, would transform our earth into Paradise. And who would want to argue about subtle terminological distinctions in such an important matter? Should [as you suggest] the purest ethical teachings be called Christianity? Why not, if this designation were useful! However, this kind of Christianity would actually be an *invisible* church—comprising Jews as well as Moslems and Chinese and counting among its members Greeks and Romans as well. It is strange how illogical we are in our judgments. When we study history, we are full of admiration for the Greeks and Romans and consider ourselves vastly inferior when we compare our virtues with theirs. Yet when we are asked to bestow upon virtue its just reward, that is, eternal salvation, we either completely disregard pagans or disdainfully dismiss them from consideration.

I was slightly taken aback by your question as to why I do not try to make proselytes. The obligation to convert others obviously follows directly from the principle that there can be no salvation outside the church of the converter. However, as a Jew,

I have no need to accept this doctrine, for according to the teachings of our rabbis (which I had quoted in my correspondence with Mr. Lavater), the righteous of all faiths can surely be saved. This principle eliminates any motive for proselytizing on our part. In fact, it obligates me not to speak ill publicly of any religion in which there is some moral good. "La religion," you say, "est le culte de Dieu." Certainly. Worship, however, as everyone knows, can be private as well as public, internal as well as external, and one does well to differentiate between the two.

The internal worship of the Jew is not based on any principles except those of *natural religion*. To spread these is, indeed, incumbent upon us, and I try to fulfill this obligation to the best of my ability. It would be very uncharitable on my part not to acknowledge this obligation, though its fulfillment is occasionally limited by certain reservations.

Our external worship, however, is in no way meant to address itself to others, since it consists of rules and prescriptions that are related to specific persons, times, and circumstances. I grant we believe that our religion is the best, because we consider it to be divinely inspired. Nevertheless, it does not follow from this premise that it is *absolutely* the best. It is the best religion for ourselves and our descendants, the best for certain times, circumstances, and conditions.

The kind of external worship that might be best for other people, God may conceivably have made known to them through prophets, or He may have enabled them to work it out by their own reasoning power. I know nothing about this issue and cannot comment on it. But I do know that no external worship can be universal; and I would be going far beyond the limits of my fathers' religion if I attempted to make proselytes.

And I know something else: that I honestly love all friends of virtue and wisdom and that I wholeheartedly admire you, dear Sir, if indeed you are what you appear to be in your letter.

From a letter to an unknown addressee
(written during the controversy with Lavater),
August 20, 1770.

A RELIGION
OF REASON

A RELIGION
WITHOUT DOGMA?

WE HAVE NO doctrines that are contrary to reason. We added nothing to natural religion save commandments and statutes. But the fundamental tenets of our religion rest on the foundation of reason. They are in consonance with the results of free inquiry, without any conflict or contradiction.

From a letter to Elkan Herz,[54]
July 23, 1771.

The sole purpose of the divine word was to single Israel out from among all other nations as God's special possession, to become holy unto Him before all other nations. With regard to the teachings of reason, however, there is no distinction between Israel and any other people.

Biur to Exodus 20.

Contemporary Judaism, like Judaism in earlier times, actually has no symbols of faith. Very few doctrines or tenets are prescribed for us. Maimonides counts thirteen of them, Albo only three; yet no one will accuse him [Albo] of heresy for that reason. We are free with regard to our doctrines. Where the opinions of the rabbis are divided, every Jew, whether uneducated or a scholar, is free to agree with the one or the other. *Elu v'elu divrei elohim chayim* ["these as well as those are the words of the living God"], say our rabbis wisely in such cases, even though this dictum is ridiculed by some who do not grasp its meaning and believe it denies the [validity of the] *principium contradictionis.* The Christians have now begun to realize how much bloodshed could have been avoided had they been guided by this saying at all times. The spirit of Judaism is conformity in deeds and freedom of thought in doctrinal matters—save for a few doctrines which are fundamental, on which all our teachers are in agreement and without which the Jewish religion simply could not exist.

From a letter to Abraham Nathan Wolf,[55]
July 11, 1782.

ON THE IMMORTALITY
OF THE SOUL

I AM DEEPLY convinced that I cannot reject the doctrine of the immortality of the soul and of retribution after death . . . without rejecting what I have always considered to be true and good. If our soul is mortal, then reason is a dream sent to us by Jupiter in order to deceive us poor mortals; then virtue is deprived of the radiance which makes it divine in our eyes; then all that has beauty and grandeur, be it moral or physical, is no longer the image of God's perfection, for nothing that is finite and transitory can refract the radiation of God's perfection. Then we have been degraded to the lowly status of animals destined only to seek food and to perish. Then it does not matter whether my life was beautiful or shameful, whether I tried to increase the number of happy people or made people miserable. . . .

From *Phädon*, Second Dialogue, Part I.

TRADITION
AS IDEA AND
EXPERIENCE

ON THE LIMITATIONS

OF RELIGIOUS AUTHORITY

I FIND IT difficult to understand how a writer of Mr. von Dohm's keen judgment could say, "Since all other religious groups have the right to expel members either temporarily or permanently, the Jewish group should have this right, too. And if there is resistance to the rabbis' edict, it should be supported by the civil authorities."[56] All societies may have the right to expel members; religious groups do not. For it is diametrically opposed to their nature and aim, which is communal edification, the joint outpouring of the heart to manifest our thankfulness to God for the numerous bounties He bestows upon us, the expression of our filial trust in His goodness and mercy. On what grounds, then, can we deny admission to dissenters, separatists, disbelievers, or sectarians and deprive them of the benefit of this edification? For people who riot or disturb the peace, there is a law, and there are the police to enforce it. Disorderliness can and should be restrained by the secular powers. But quiet and inoffensive attendance at a religious meeting should not be forbidden even to an offender unless we deliberately want to bar him from every road to self-improvement. . . .

Mr. von Dohm claims for the Jewish religion the same privileges that are granted to all other religions. As long as these still possess the right of expulsion, he considers it an inconsistency to impose greater restrictions upon the Jewish religion. But if, as I am firmly convinced, "religious claims to worldly things," "power and compulsion in religious affairs" are meaningless phrases—and if expulsion, generally, must be considered irreligious—then let us rather be inconsistent than multiply abuses.

I do not find that the wisest of our forefathers ever claimed to possess the right to exclude individuals from religious practices.

When King Solomon had completed the Temple, he included, in his dedicatory prayer, even "strangers," a term that was synonymous with idolators in his days. He lifted his hands to heaven and said, "Moreover, concerning the stranger who is not of Thy people Israel, when he shall come out of a far country for Thy name's sake—for they shall hear of Thy great name and of Thy mighty hand and of Thine outstretched arm—when he shall come and pray toward this house; hear Thou in heaven, Thy dwelling-place, and do according to all that the stranger calleth to Thee for; that all the peoples of the earth may know Thy name, to fear Thee, as doth Thy people Israel, and that they may know that Thy name is called upon this house which I have built." In the same manner, our rabbis directed that the gifts and votive offerings of idolators be accepted in the Temple. The sacrifice even of an offender could not be rejected as long as he had not positively renounced his religion.

From the Preface to the German translation
of Manasseh ben Israel's *Vindiciae Judaeorum*,
Berlin, March 19, 1782.

ON TOLERANCE

THE DISTANT GOAL: A CHALLENGE

THE SPIRIT OF conciliation as well as of love demand that the stronger party should take the first step. He must waive his claim to superiority and make the overture if the weaker party is to gain sufficient confidence to respond. If it be the design of Providence that brethren shall love each other, it is evidently the duty of the stronger to make the first move, open his arms and cry out, like Augustus, "Let us be friends."

Previous writings and arguments about tolerance have been, however, concerned only with the three major denominations favored in the Roman empire, at best including some of their denominational branches. Pagans, Jews, Mohammedans, and deists are either not mentioned at all or only for one purpose: to question the arguments presented in favor of tolerance. "According to your premises," the opponents argue, "we must not merely . . . tolerate Jews and deists but actually permit them to share fully in the rights and obligations of mankind. . . ."

It is a strange experience to observe the different forms which prejudice has assumed through the ages in order to oppress us and frustrate our civil emancipation. In former times, rife with superstition, it was sacred things that we were said to defile wantonly; crucifixes that we stabbed and caused to bleed; children whom we secretly circumcised and mutilated to feast our eyes on their tortures; Christian blood that we used for Passover; wells

145

that we poisoned; heresy, intractability, witchcraft, the practice of fiendish magic—these were the things of which we were accused, for which we were martyred, robbed of our property, driven into exile, if not actually slain.

Now times have changed. Those calumnies no longer have the desired effect. Now we are accused of superstition and ineptitude; of lack of moral sensitivity, taste, and good manners; of being unfit for the arts, sciences, and useful trades, especially as far as they may be required for military and government service; of an irresistible disposition to fraud, usury, and the evasion of taxes. These charges are now used instead of the former cruder accusations in order to exclude us from the ranks of useful citizens and to deny us the motherly protection of the state. Formerly, people made every conceivable effort not to make us useful citizens but to make us—Christians. But since we were obstinate and stubbornly refused to be converted, they considered our refusal sufficient reason to treat us as an unwanted and useless burden on society and to ascribe to this detestable monster every infamy under the sun in order to expose us to the hatred and contempt of the rest of mankind.

Today the zeal to convert us has abated. Now we are completely neglected. We continue to be barred from the arts, the sciences, the useful trades and occupations of mankind; every avenue to improvement is blocked, while our alleged lack of refinement is used as a pretext for our further oppression. They tie our hands and then reproach us for not using them. . . .

Until now, all the nations of the earth seem to have suffered from the delusion that religion can be maintained by iron force; that doctrines of holiness can be inculcated by unholy persecution; that true notions of God who, as we all acknowledge, is love itself, can be communicated by hatred and ill will. You have probably permitted yourselves to be misled and to adopt the same views. The power to persecute others seems to have become the most important privilege that your persecutors could bestow upon you. Thank the God of your fathers, who is the God of all love and mercy, that this delusion is gradually vanishing. Nations are now tolerating one another; they show a measure of kindness and forbearance toward you—an attitude which, with the help of Him who fashions the hearts of men, may ultimately grow into genuine brotherly love. Oh, my brethren, follow the example of love, just as you formerly followed that of hatred. Emulate the virtues of the nations whose vices you had previously felt impelled to imitate. If you would desire protection, tolerance, and sufferance from others, then protect, tolerate, and suffer each other. *Love, and you will be loved.*

> From the Preface to the German translation of the *Vindiciae Judaeorum* of Manasseh ben Israel,[57] Berlin, March 19, 1782.

WHAT IS TRUE TOLERANCE?

With regard to tolerance, which is so strongly advocated in all newspapers, I have by no means the same favorable opinion that you have evidenced. As long as [the desire to establish] a systematic union of faiths is lurking hidden in the background, this tolerance is a sham that seems to me more dangerous than open persecution. Montesquieu, if I am not mistaken, in his *Lettres persanes*, has already expressed the destructive view that the best method of conversion is not harshness and persecution but kindness and tolerance; and I have the impression that this principle, and not wisdom and love of one's fellowman, is seeking to become the dominant approach. In this case, it would be even more necessary for the small band of those who do not wish to convert others or be converted themselves to keep together and close ranks—and by what means? I am once again led to [affirm] the necessity of the ceremonial law, lest doctrines will be transformed into laws. . . .

> From a letter to Herz Homberg,[58] March 1, 1784.

ON THE MEANING
OF THE LAW

RITUAL LAW AS UNIFYING BOND

I REALIZE THAT we do not agree on the necessity of ritual laws. They may have lost their significance and usefulness as script or sign language. But their necessity as a unifying bond of our people has not been lost. And this unifying bond will, I believe, have to be preserved in the plans of Providence as long as polytheism, anthropomorphism, and religious usurpation are rampant in the world. As long as these tormentors of reason are united against us, genuine theists must also create some kind of unifying bond among themselves lest the others gain the upper hand completely. But of what should this bond consist? Of principles and beliefs? We would then get articles of faith, symbols, doctrinal formulas—all shackling our reason. It is of acts that the bond must consist, and of meaningful acts at that—i.e., ceremonies. All our efforts should actually have only one goal: to eliminate the far-reaching abuses of the ceremonies and to endow them with genuine and real meaning.

From a letter to Herz Homberg,
September 22, 1783.

THE VALUE OF THE LAW

God has given us many commandments without revealing their purpose to us. However, it should be sufficient for us to know that they were commanded by Him. Inasmuch as we have to take the yoke of His dominion upon us, we are obligated to do His will. Their value lies in their practice, not in the understanding of their origin or purpose.

Biur to Exodus 23:19.

CONTINUITY AND CHANGE IN THE LAW

As far as popular religious notions are concerned, it seems to me that the pleasant emotions they evoke from us are largely founded on some underlying truths dimmed through false accretions. . . . Therefore, I adhere to the popular religious notions as long as my reason is unable to provide a substitute for these pleasant emotions.

From a letter to Sophie Becker,[59]
December 27, 1785.

A NEW BIBLE
TRANSLATION [60]

WHY A NEW BIBLE TRANSLATION?

IN 1544 the great grammarian Rabbi Elijah Bachur (Elijah Levita)[61] translated the Torah and the Five Scrolls word by word into German. His translation was published in Constance, in Switzerland. A later German translation, printed in Hebrew letters, was published by Rabbi Joel Witzenhausen in Amsterdam in 1679 (second edition in 1687). In the same year, still another German translation by Rabbi Jekutiel Blitz, of Witmund, appeared in Amsterdam, containing approbations as well as admonitions [against unauthorized reprinting] by several eminent rabbis of his time. In his preface, Rabbi Jekutiel criticizes the Constance translation vigorously and says he is convinced that it could not possibly have been the work of the illustrious grammarian Elijah Bachur. I myself have never seen the translation attributed to Rabbi Elijah, since copies are not available in this country. However, I have seen Rabbi Jekutiel's translation and find that he has made himself ridiculous [by criticizing faults in others of which he himself is not free]. His ability is very limited. He neither understands the spirit of the Hebrew language nor masters its use; and whatever little he did understand, he rendered into a language so corrupt and garbled that any reader who is accustomed to precise usage must find it disgusting.

Since that time, no one has attempted to improve what had been corrupted and to translate the Holy Torah into the kind of language that would be appropriate for our time. The Jewish boys who are able to understand and probe its wisdom must acquire their knowledge of God's word from translations prepared by Christian scholars. Christians have translated the Torah repeatedly and into various languages, in accordance with the needs of the times and changes in style and linguistic usage. Sometimes they translated literally, sometimes in paraphrases; sometimes they were faithful to the text, and sometimes they rendered its general meaning in order to satisfy the needs and desires of every reader. . . .

But to follow this procedure is hardly appropriate for the people of Israel. For us, the Torah is and must be considered a source of law. To make sure that our life's purpose and direction should not be dependent on subtle and frequently changing interpretations and speculations, our wise ancestors have established the Masorah, thereby erecting a fence around the Torah and the law, so that we would not have to tap around in darkness like blind men. From this established path we may not turn right or left, nor may we follow the opinions or hypotheses of this or that grammarian or critic of the text. Our sole guiding principle must be the text itself that the Masoretes have established for us. . . .

God has blessed me with boys. And when the time had come to instruct them in the Torah and to teach them the living word of God as it is contained in the Holy Scriptures, I began, for the benefit of my youngsters, to translate the Five Books of Moses into the pure and correct German that is our vernacular today. I acquainted them with the original text. In addition, however, I taught them the translation, which was sometimes literal and sometimes based on the meaning and context of a phrase.

In this way I wanted them to acquire an appreciation of the spirit of the Holy Scriptures, of the subtleties of their language, of their poetry and beauty—all in the hope that they would be able to continue their studies on their own as they grew older. God then brought Rabbi Solomon of Dubno to me, and he instructed the only son who had been spared unto me (may God strengthen him and incline his heart to His service) in Hebrew grammar for an hour every day. When he saw my translation of the Torah, he liked it and considered it adequate. He urged me to have it printed for the benefit of other students whom God had endowed with linguistic interest and talent. I agreed, but only under the condition that he himself would put his heart and mind to the task of preparing a commentary in order to explain and justify my translation—e.g., why, in certain instances, I had preferred the views of an older commentator to someone else's, why I had occasionally ignored the explanation of other commentators altogether and had instead provided an explanation of my own. . .

From the Introduction to the translation of the Pentateuch, 1778.

A FIRST STEP TO CULTURE

According to the initial plan for my future, as I had outlined it during my better years, I certainly never intended to become a publisher or translator of the Bible. I wanted to limit myself to supervising the production of silk goods by day, while I hoped to derive some enjoyment from the pursuit of philosophy during my hours of leisure. However, it pleased Providence to lead me on an entirely different course. As a result of Lavater's imposition, I lost the capacity for quiet contemplation and, with it, my peace of mind. After some deliberation, I found that the remainder of my energy would still suffice to render a service to my children and perhaps even to a considerable number of my people, if I provided them with a better translation and explanation of the Holy Scriptures than those available until now. This is the first step to culture from which, alas, my nation has held itself so aloof that one might almost despair of any possibility of improvement. Nevertheless, I felt it was my obligation to do whatever little I could and to leave the rest to Providence, which often takes more time to carry out its plan than we can anticipate.

From a letter to August von Hennings,[62]
Strelitz, June 29, 1779.

EDUCATION—FOR WHAT?

I, too, have children whom I am to educate. For what destiny?
. . . My duty is to educate them in such a way that they will not bring disgrace upon themselves in any situation and that they will be able to endure, with resignation, the disgrace heaped upon them undeservedly by their neighbors. This was the purpose of my translation, at least in its initial stages.

From a letter to Herder,[63]
Berlin, June 20, 1780.

FOR RABBIS AS WELL AS THE COMMON MAN

If my translation were to be accepted by all Jews, without any objection, it would be superfluous. But the more the so-called savants of our time oppose it, the more sorely it is needed. I had originally prepared it for the common man alone; but now I feel that rabbis need it even worse, and I should like, with the help of God, to publish a translation of the Prophets and the Hagiographa as well.

From a letter to Henoch,
Berlin, March 30, 1780.

THE PRINCIPLES OF
JUDAISM—A CREDO

As FAR AS its major tenets are concerned, the religion of my fathers knows no mysteries which we have to accept on faith rather than comprehend. Our intellect can quite comfortably start out from the well-established primary principles of human cognition and be sure that it will eventually encounter religion on the same road. Here is no conflict between religion and reason, no rebellion of our natural cognitive faculty against the stifling authority of faith. "Its ways are ways of pleasantness, and all its paths are peace."

Essentially, the religion of the Israelites encompasses only three central principles: *God, Providence*, and *legislation*. These principles were expanded by our religious leaders along the following lines:

(*a*) God, the Author and absolute Sovereign of all things, is one and simple [single] (in His person as well as His nature).

(*b*) This God is aware of all that happens in His creation. He rewards good and punishes evil by natural and, at times, by supranatural means.

(*c*) This God has made known His laws to the children of Israel through Moses, the son of Amram. We still possess these laws in writing.

We believe that man was created in the image of God but that he was, nevertheless, also meant to be man—inclined to sin. We

154

recognize no original sin. Adam and Eve sinned because they were human. They died because they had sinned. This is the condition of all their descendants. . . .

However, they die only physically. I recognize no death of the soul. True, Maimonides,[64] writing on repentance, makes the assumption that the soul of the godless must perish, and he rightfully considers this the harshest punishment that is possible.[65] I, however, agree with Nachmanides,[66] who rejects this doctrine in his tractate on retribution and denies that the soul can perish and that punishment can be everlasting. . . .

God punishes the sinner not according to His own infinity but according to the sinner's frailty. We know of no lese majesty which wants or has to be avenged. We know of no criminal judgment that must be executed—if not against the guilty party, then against the innocent person who voluntarily takes this suffering upon himself. While, according to our views, it is unjust to spare the guilty, it is even more unjust to let the innocent suffer. Even though he may wish to take suffering upon himself out of compassion, supreme wisdom cannot approve of it, and justice (that is, all-wise grace) cannot be satisfied by such self-imposed suffering. . . .

We believe the laws of Moses are strictly binding upon us as long as God does not revoke them explicitly and with the same public solemnity with which He has given them. Is their purpose no longer completely known to us? Granted. But where did the Legislator declare that they should be binding only as long as we know their purpose? And what mortal would be presumptuous enough to limit their validity without such a divine declaration? Human laws can be changed by men in response to changing times and circumstances. But divine laws remain unalterable until we can be utterly sure that God himself has announced a change.

Will God ever change these laws? On this point, our scholars are of divided opinion. Some consider them absolutely immutable and insist that this position represents one of Judaism's central doctrines. Others do not consider it unlikely that the supreme Legislator may plan a second public giving of the law in connection with some future miraculous restoration of the Jewish nation. In this case, many of our present ceremonial laws might undergo changes. My views in this matter are based on the following considerations:

I have said repeatedly that, in the opinion of all our rabbis, the Mosaic laws are binding only upon the Jewish people and that all other peoples are merely required to abide by the law of nature and the religion of the patriarchs. However, most peoples have deviated from the simplicity of this first religion and, to the detriment of truth, have evolved false notions of God and His sovereignty. Therefore, it seems that the ceremonial laws of the Jews have, among other unfathomable reasons, the additional purpose of making this people stand out from among all other nations and reminding it, through a variety of religious acts, perpetually of the sacred truths that none of us should ever forget. This is undoubtedly the purpose of most religious customs. Clear and explicit evidence for this view can be found in our Holy Scriptures. These customs are to remind us that God is one; that He has created the world and reigns over it in wisdom; that He is the absolute Lord over all of nature; that He has liberated this people by extraordinary deeds from Egyptian oppression; that He has given them laws, etc. This is the purpose of all the customs that we observe, though they must necessarily seem superfluous, cumbersome, and ludicrous to all who do not understand their meaning.

Now, all prophets of the Old Testament are agreed, and reason fully concurs in this hope, that the difference between religions will not last forever, that ultimately there will be one shepherd and one flock, and that the acknowledgment of the true God will cover the earth as the waters cover the sea. At that time, divine wisdom may no longer find it necessary to set us apart from other peoples by special ceremonial laws. In fact, it might choose a second public manifestation to introduce ritual observances that will link the hearts of *all* men in adoration of their Creator and in mutual love and benevolence.

From *Bonnet's Palingenesis:
A Counterinquiry*.

NOTES—
SOURCES—
GUIDE FOR
FURTHER READING

NOTES

1. For a more detailed treatment of Mendelssohn's life and work, see "Moses Mendelssohn," by Alfred Jospe, in *Great Jewish Personalities in Modern Times*, ed. by Simon Noveck, Washington, D.C., 1960, 11–36. Permission to utilize portions of this material is gratefully acknowledged.

2. *Jerusalem*, published in 1783, was written in response to a challenge presented in an anonymous pamphlet entitled *The Search for Light and Right*, 1782. The pamphlet's author was the Austrian convert Joseph von Sonnenfels. A postcript was written by David Ernst Mörschel, an army chaplain in Berlin. See Jacob Katz, "To Whom Was Mendelssohn Replying in *Jerusalem?*" (in Hebrew), *Zion*, XXXIX, 1–2, 1964, 112–132.

3. Jacob Emden (1697–1776), also called Yaabetz (an abbreviation of Yaacov ben Zevi)—rabbi, talmudic scholar, polemicist, and author—lived in Altona (Germany), then under the rule of Denmark. Mendelssohn's letter (in Hebrew) was written October 26, 1773 (*GSJA*, XVI, 178).

JERUSALEM

[Hereafter, except where indicated as *Ed.*, the notes are Mendelssohn's.]

4. Bellarmine himself was in danger of being called a heretic by Pope Sixtus V for ascribing to him only indirect power over the temporal domain of kings and princes. His work was placed on the *Index*. [Robert Cardinal Bellarmine, 1542–1621; his chief work is *Disputationes de controversiis Christianae fidei*, 3 vols., 1586–1589. *Ed.*]

5. Cf. note to Abbt's "Friendly Correspondence," p. 28.

6. Cf. *Abot*, IV, 21: "This world is a vestibule of the world to come; prepare yourself in the vestibule so that you may enter the hall" [*Ed.*].

7. One may object that a soldier in a war has the right to kill the enemy, while the enemy does not have the duty to submit to this fate. However, the soldier has this right not as a human being but as a mercenary, a member of the warring state. The state either is or claims to be offended, so that it can seek satisfaction only by the use of force. The conflict, therefore, is not actually between man and man but between state and state. Obviously, only one of the two warring states can be right. However, it is the duty of the offending party to give satisfaction to the offended and to suffer all that is necessary to restore the impaired right of the offended.

8. When two persons of different religions marry, the principles that will govern their household and determine their children's upbringing are contractually agreed upon. What, however, if husband or wife changes his or her religious views after marriage and converts to another religion? Does such a step entitle the other party to demand a divorce? A small publication (*The Search for Light and Right*, published by Friedrich Maurer, Berlin, 1782), supposedly written in Vienna (I shall have occasion to refer to it again in my second chapter), reports that such a case has actually happened there. A Jew who was converted to Christianity is reported to have insisted that he be permitted to keep his wife, who has remained Jewish. Legal action has reportedly been instituted. The author of the publication judges the case in accordance with the "statute of freedom." "It can rightfully be assumed," he says, "that a difference of religion is not a valid cause for divorce. According to the principles of our wise

ruler [Emperor Joseph II], disagreement in religious views cannot be used to invalidate a social contract."

A rash conclusion, I would think. I hope an Emperor who is as just as he is wise will also listen to the counterarguments and will not permit the statute of freedom to be used for oppression and violence. If marriage is merely a civil contract—and it cannot be anything else between two Jewish partners, even by Catholic principles—the wording and conditions of the contract must be interpreted and defined in accordance with the intent of the contracting parties rather than that of the legislator or judge. If we have reason to assume that the contracting parties, in accordance with their convictions, did understand and, had they been asked, would have interpreted certain wordings in a particular way, this interpretation—morally certain and accepted as a tacit precondition of the contract—ought to be as valid before the court as if it had been an explicit agreement.

Now, inasmuch as both partners were at least formally still Jewish when they entered into the marriage contract, it is obvious that they intended to establish a Jewish home and to raise their children in the Jewish faith. The partner who took her religion seriously certainly could not have assumed anything else; and she would surely not have taken any other position even if she had been able to anticipate such a fundamental change, or if such a possibility had been discussed between the partners. All she knew and expected was to start out in a home governed by tradition and to bear children who would be raised according to her ancestral principles. If the difference of religion is important to her, and if it is a matter of record that such a difference must indeed have been important to her when she entered into the marriage contract, the contract must then be defined in terms of *her* understanding and views. And even if the whole country were to view this matter differently, it still could not affect the interpretation of the contract. The husband is changing his convictions and adopting another religion. If his wife were forced to accept a domestic arrangement to which her conscience objects, if, in one word, she were compelled to accept conditions of the marriage contract to which she had never agreed—she would obviously suffer an injustice. And we, in turn, would just as obviously be permitting ourselves to deny someone's freedom of conscience while simultaneously pretending that we are safeguarding it. The conditions of the contract can no longer be fulfilled. The husband, having converted, is at least culpable (*in culpa*), though not guilty of deception (*in dolo*): he is responsible for the fact that these conditions can no longer be fulfilled. Should the wife's freedom of conscience be restricted because her husband wants to have freedom of conscience? When did she agree to that? Should her conscience not also be free, and should the party that caused the change not take responsibility for its consequences and therefore indemnify and, as far as possible, reinstate the other party in her former situation? Nothing, it seems to me, could be simpler. The issue is clear. Nobody can be forced to accept contractual conditions to which he cannot agree as a matter of principle.

Both partners have equal rights concerning their children's education. If we had nondenominational educational institutions, the children of such disputed cases could be brought up impartially until they reach the age of reason and can make their own choice. But as long as we cannot make such arrangements, and as long as our educational institutions are still connected with specific religious traditions, the partner who remains true to his original principles and does not change them should clearly have the prerogative to educate the children. This, too, follows naturally from the above-mentioned principles, and nothing but flagrant presumption and religious oppression would occur if the opposite view were ever enforced. Our ruler, Joseph, who is as wise as he is just, would surely not permit such violent abuse of the power of the church in his realm.

9. In the development of this, to me, quite convincing definition of terms and concepts, I was guided by the philosopher and jurist Assistant Counselor Klein, a dear friend with whom I have had the pleasure of discussing this material. I believe this theory of contracts is as simple as it is fruitful. In his work *Moral Philosophy*, Fergouson, as well as his excellent translator, deduces the necessity of keeping a promise from the *expectation* aroused in

our fellowman and from the immorality inherent in *deception*. From these factors, however, we can at most deduce a duty of conscience. Whatever portion of my goods I was originally conscience-bound to relinquish for the benefit of my fellowmen in general, I am now conscience-bound to relinquish for the benefit of some particular individual whose expectations I have aroused. But how is this duty of conscience to be transformed into a compulsory obligation? To explain this transformation, I think the above-mentioned principles pertaining to cession in general and to the rights of decision involved in conflict of interests in particular are indispensable.

10. The terms "service," "honor," etc., have different meanings depending on whether they are used in relation to God or in relation to man. "Serving" God is not a service which is rendered to God; "honoring" God is not an honor which I accord to God. The meaning of these words has been changed in order to preserve their use. But the common man still clings to the meaning with which he is familiar and persists in his use of a terminology that has caused enormous confusion in religious matters.

11. The psalmist sings, "Sacrifice and meal-offering Thou hast no delight in; mine ears hast Thou opened" [Ps. 40:7]. [In most cases Mendelssohn's own rendering of Scripture is translated; otherwise Old Testament references are taken from the Jewish Publication Society Version, New Testament references, from the Revised Standard Version. *Ed.*]

12. *Talmud Babli*, Chagigah, 7*a* [*Ed.*].

13. Some time ago, a society of highly learned and respected men in a very tolerant country compelled dissidents to pay double fees for their professional approbation. When their action was challenged by the authorities, their excuse was that the dissidents were evil in civil life *deterioris conditionis* ["of inferior condition"]. Strangely enough, their higher fees are said to be in effect even now.

14. Pierre Bayle (1647–1706), French critic; one of the founders of eighteenth-century rationalism [*Ed.*]

15. A contractual stipulation is valid and binding if it could possibly have influenced the decision in cases involving the colli-

sion of property rights. But I doubt whether mere influence can ever be considered to be a legally valid stipulation or whether it is not simply erroneously thought to involve or produce material advantages.

16. *Talmud Babli*, Baba Batra, 16a [*Ed.*].

17. Christian Wilhelm von Dohm (1741–1828), military counselor to Frederick the Great. See note 56 [*Ed.*].

18. In the preface to Manasseh ben Israel's *Salvation of the Jews* [*Ed.*].

19. The words of my late friend, Mr. Iselin, in one of his last essays in *The Ephemerides of Mankind*. The memory of this wise man should be unforgettable to all of his contemporaries who cherish integrity and truth. Therefore, I find it incomprehensible how I could have omitted his name when I listed the benevolent men who had been the first to attempt to promote the principles of unlimited tolerance in Germany—a man who had proclaimed them earlier and more emphatically in our language than anyone else. It is therefore with special pleasure that I include here the following quotation from the announcement of my introduction to Rabbi Manasseh in *The Ephemerides* (No. 10, October 1782, p. 429), where the subject is mentioned, in order to do justice, at least posthumously, to a man whose entire life had been characterized by utter fairness and integrity:

The author of *The Ephemerides of Mankind* agrees entirely with what Mr. Mendelssohn says about the factors which limit the legislative power of the authorities with regard to the private views of citizens and the agreements into which individuals can enter regarding these views. Moreover, he has not held this position merely since the publication of Mr. von Dohm's and Mr. Lessing's writings, but he had already professed it more than thirty years ago. Similarly, he had recognized already many years ago that so-called religious tolerance is not a favor bestowed by the government but its obligation. No one could have expressed this view more pointedly than he did when he wrote (in *Dreams of a Humanitarian*, Vol. II, pp. 12 and 13), "Should one or several religions become established in his domain, a wise and just sovereign will not permit himself to impair their rights to his own advantage. Any church, any association, whose purpose it is to worship God is a society entitled to the protection and justice of the sovereign. To withhold them even if it were done in order to favor and promote the best religion would be contrary to the spirit of true godliness."

As far as their civil rights are concerned, the adherents of all religions are equal, with the sole exception of those whose beliefs run counter to the fundamental rules governing human and civil conduct. Such beliefs can obviously not claim any right in the state, and those who are unfortunate enough to hold these beliefs can expect toleration only as long as they do not disturb the social order by unjust or harmful acts. If they do, they must be punished, not for their beliefs but for their actions.

There is, however, a factual error in the passage preceding this statement (p. 423) in which I am said to have—wrongly—imputed certain views about the role of intermediaries to the author of *The Ephemerides*. It was not Mr. Iselin but another, otherwise quite discerning, author, who had published an essay in *The Ephemerides* in which he asserted the harmfulness of intermediaries—a thesis which was refuted by the publisher himself.

I am not going to comment on the references to my coreligionists that were made in the announcement. This is not the place to defend them. I leave this business to Mr. von Dohm, who can take care of it with greater impartiality. Besides, it is quite easy to forgive a citizen of Basel for his prejudice against a people that he could possibly have come to know only by an occasional contact with some of its itinerant members or by reading about it in the *Observations d'un Alsacien*.

20. The man who holds the office of circumciser among Jews enjoys neither an income nor a special rank in the congregation. On the contrary, whoever has the requisite skill performs this meritorious task gladly. Indeed, the father whose religious duty it would actually be to circumcise his son must often choose among several applicants for the performance of this religious act. The only reward which the man who performs it may accept is a seat at the head of the table during the meal following the circumcision and the privilege of saying grace after the meal. If

only all religious positions were similarly filled according to my seemingly new and harsh theory!

21. See *The Search for Light and Right*, in a letter to Mr. M. Mendelssohn, Berlin, 1782 [*Ed.*].

22. The word "all" is an interpolation by Mendelssohn and is not contained in the original Hebrew text [*Ed.*].

23. Gotthold Ephraim Lessing (1729–1781), German dramatist and literary critic and one of the most influential literary figures of his time. Lessing was Mendelssohn's close friend and mentor. His critical writings include *Litteraturbriefe*, 1759–1765, and *Laocoön*, 1776. Among his dramatic works are *Minna von Barnhelm*, 1767, *Emilia Galotti*, 1779, and especially, *Nathan der Weise*, 1779 [*Ed.*].

24. Moses Maimonides (1135–1204), religious philosopher and codifier, author of *Moreh Nebuchim* ("Guide to the Perplexed") and *Mishneh Torah*, a codification of Jewish law [*Ed.*].

25. "Magnified be . . . ," composed in medieval Italy, the hymn became a part of the daily worship [*Ed.*].

26. Chasdai Crescas (Spain, 14–15th cent.), author of *Or Adonai* ("The Light of God"). His disciple Joseph Albo (Spain, 14–15th cent.) wrote *Ikkarim* ("Principles"); the three principles of Judaism are the existence of God, revelation, and reward and punishment. Isaac Abarbanel (Spain, 15–16th cent.), statesman and Bible commentator. Herbert of Cherbury (16–17th cent.), English deist. Isaac Luria (16th cent.), head of the Safed (Palestine) group of Jewish mystics [*Ed.*].

27. *Talmud Babli*, Erubin, 13*b*. I have seen many pedants use this saying to prove that our rabbis do not believe in the principle of contradiction [*principium contradictionis*]. I hope I shall still see the day when all nations of the earth will recognize the validity of the following exception to the principle of contradiction: "The fast of the fourth month, and the fast of the fifth, and the fast of the seventh, and the fast of the tenth, shall be to the house of Judah joy and gladness, and cheerful seasons . . ." [Zech. 8:19].

28. *Talmud Babli*, Shabbat, 31*a* [*Ed.*].

29. *Ibid.*, Berachot, 54*a* [*Ed.*].

30. Albrecht von Haller (1708–1777), Swiss physiologist, anatomist, and author [*Ed.*].

31. Here Mendelssohn quotes some examples which we do not reproduce [*Ed.*].

32. Christoph Meiners (1747–1810), professor in Göttingen; philosopher and historian of religion [*Ed.*].

33. I.e., the words "God, all-wise, all-powerful, all-good, rewards the good."

34. A secondary school in Dessau, founded by Prof. Basedow *et al.* about 1770 [*Ed.*].

35. *History of the Sciences in Greece and Rome*, II, p. 77 [in German].

36. What a profound thought: You wanted to behold all My glory. I will let all My *goodness* pass before you. You will see it only from behind. Mortal eyes cannot discern it from the front.

37. Mendelssohn quotes from his German translation of the Pentateuch [*Ed.*].

38. The content of this entire psalm is extremely important. Interested readers will do well to read it in its entirety with close attention and to compare it with my remarks above. It seems obvious to me that the psalm was inspired by this remarkable passage in Scripture and that it is nothing but an outburst of great emotion evoked from the singer by his contemplation of this extraordinary event. At the beginning of the psalm, he therefore summons his soul to solemn thanksgiving for God's promise of grace and fatherly mercy: "Bless the Lord, O my soul, and all that is within me, bless His holy name. Bless the Lord, O my soul, and forget not all His benefits; Who forgiveth all thine iniquity; Who healeth all thy diseases; Who redeems thy life from the pit; Who encompasseth thee with loving-kindness and tender mercies," etc.

39. Cf. *Talmud Babli*, Sanhedrin, 46*b*, Makkot, 7*a* [*Ed.*].

40. *Ibid.*, Shabbat, 15*a* [*Ed.*].

41. See note 56 [*Ed.*].

42. Atheism, too, has its fanaticism, as painful experience teaches. Fanaticism can probably never go on a rampage unless it is associated with a deep conviction that there is no God. Nevertheless, that even a superficial kind of athesim can become fanat-

ical is as undeniable as it is difficult to understand. The avowed atheist must act exclusively from selfishness in order to be consistent. This hardly seems to be the case when he attempts to enlist the support of others for his views instead of keeping the secret to himself. And yet one can hear him preach his doctrines with the most intensive zeal. In fact, he has been seen to rave and even to persecute if his sermons did not find a favorable reception. Zealousness is something terrible when it takes possession of an avowed atheist—when innocence becomes the victim of a raving tyrant who fears all things but God.

43. Alas, we can hear even the American Congress intone the old song once again when it speaks of a "dominant religion."

COVENANTS—OLD AND NEW

44. Johann Caspar Lavater (1741–1801), pastor in Zurich and author, among other writings, of *Physiognomische Fragmente*, 1774–1787. During a visit to Berlin in 1763, Lavater, then twenty-two years old, met Mendelssohn and had several conversations with him. Lavater was deeply impressed by Mendelssohn and concluded from the respectful way in which he spoke of the founder of Christianity that the Jewish philosopher might be ripe for conversion. Six years later, when Charles Bonnet (see note 51) published his *La palingénésie philosophique, ou idées sur l'état passé et sur l'état futur des êtres vivants*, Lavater, impressed by Bonnet's arguments, prepared a German translation of the second part of Bonnet's work in which the author attempted to demonstrate the historical truth of Christianity and dedicated the translation to Mendelssohn, challenging him to refute Bonnet's arguments publicly or to do "what a Socrates would have done had he read the treatise and found it irrefutable."

Lavater rushed an unbound copy of his translation to Mendelssohn, which arrived on September 4, 1769. The dedicatory inscription caused consternation in Berlin as well as in Zurich (*GSJA*, VII, Introduction, xix). Mendelssohn published his reply, *Schreiben an den Herrn Diaconus Lavater zu Zürich,* on December 12, 1769, and sent a copy, together with a covering letter, to Lavater twelve days later. Lavater had, however, written to Mendelssohn on December 26 (before the *Schreiben* could reach him) to apologize for his ill-considered action. Mendelssohn responded a few weeks later. In the meantime, however, Lavater had already drafted *his* reply, *Antwort an den Herrn Moses Mendelssohn zu Berlin,* and sent it to Berlin for publication. Mendelssohn, in turn, responded in a *Nacherinnerung,* probably written in March 1770 [*Ed.*].

45. Cf. *Talmud Babli,* Sanhedrin, 59a; Maimonides, *Mishneh Torah,* Hilchot Melachim, VIII, 10 [*Ed.*].

46. The seven Noachide laws, which embody the basic elements of natural law, require man to refrain from idolatry, adultery and incest, bloodshed, robbery, social injustice, and eating flesh from a living animal. Cf. *Talmud Babli,* Abodah Zarah, 64b; see also Maimonides, *op. cit.,* Hilchot Melachim, IX, X [*Ed.*].

47. *Hasidei umot ha-olam.* Maimonides adds the limitation that this is true only if they observe the Noachide laws not merely as a requirement of natural law but as laws specifically promulgated by God. However, the talmudic text does not imply this limitation.

48. Maimonides [*op. cit.*], Hilchot Teshuvah, III, 5; Hilchot Melachim, VIII, 11. In a letter to Rabbi Hasdai Halevi, Maimonides said, "As far as all other people are concerned, I want you to know, dear friend, that God looks only into the heart of men and judges their actions in accordance with their conscience. Therefore, our sages teach that the righteous of all nations are entitled to eternal salvation, insofar as they seek God and practice virtue."

Manasseh ben Israel, in his treatise *Nishmat Hayyim,* quotes decisive statements from the Talmud, the Zohar, and other texts that demonstrate this doctrine beyond the possibility of any doubt. The author of Kosri [i.e., the *Kuzari*] states that "we do not want to deprive any human being of his merited reward." Rabbi Jacob Hirschel, one of the most erudite spiritual leaders of our time, discusses this issue extensively in several of his writings.

49. See Maimonides, *op. cit.*, Hilchot Issure Biah, XIII, XIV [*Ed.*].

50. Jean François Marmontel (1723–1799), French dramatist, critic, and contributor to the *Encyclopédie* [*Ed.*].

51. This essay was published anonymously in London in 1755 under the title *Essai de psychologie, ou considérations sur les opérations de l'âmé sur l'habitude et sur l'éducation*. Lavater believed the author was a certain M. Tourneyser of Basel, Switzerland. Mendelssohn assumed (erroneously) that this essay was by some anonymous author who had influenced Bonnet's views significantly. However, most scholars today assume that it was actually written by Bonnet himself, although he continued to insist quite stoutly that he was not the author. For an extensive analysis of this problem, see *GSJA*, VII, 457 [*Ed.*].

52. Karl-Wilhem, Hereditary Prince and later Duke of Braunschweig-Wolfenbüttel (1735–1806), wrote to Mendelssohn on January 2, 1770, that he had derived great pleasure from reading the third edition of Mendelssohn's *Phädon* as well as his letter to Lavater. He praised Mendelssohn's sensitivity and humanity, to which every word of his writing testified, but urged Mendelssohn at the same time to clarify two questions that puzzled him: first, on what grounds a thinker who observes the Mosaic law can prove the historicity of the Old Testament, yet reject that of the New Testament; second, on what grounds he rejects the proofs for the Christian faith recorded in the Old Testament as divinely revealed, even according to Jewish tradition.

The exact date of Mendelssohn's answer is not known. He probably responded shortly after he had received the Prince's letter. Cf. *GSJA*, VII, p. xciv [*Ed.*].

53. Charles Bonnet (1720–1793) French philosopher and psychologist, was the author of *La palingénésie philosophique, ou idées sur l'état passé et sur l'état futur des êtres vivants*, 1769. Bonnet criticized Lavater for the way he had challenged Mendelssohn (see note 44), and he wrote to Mendelssohn directly to assure him that he, Bonnet, had not instigated Lavater's act. At the

same time he asked for Mendelssohn's critical comment on his treatise.

Mendelssohn probably drafted his *Gegenbetrachtungen* (*Counterinquiry*) in 1769 or early in 1770. However, they were not published at that time. Mendelssohn merely wanted to be prepared in case he would have to debate the issue publicly with Bonnet. The draft represents Mendelssohn's first systematic, though in many ways still fragmentary, attempt to examine and clarify the issues which later found their mature formulation and exposition in *Jerusalem* [*Ed.*].

A RELIGION OF REASON

54. A wealthy merchant and relative of Mendelssohn's [*Ed.*].

55. Abraham Nathan Wolf (1751–1784) of Dessau, author of a textbook on Jewish religion and a commentary on the Book of Job; a scholar much appreciated by Mendelssohn [*Ed.*].

TRADITION AS IDEA AND EXPERIENCE

56. In 1779 the Jews of Alsace were attacked in a pamphlet written by a French judge. The leaders of the Jewish communities wanted to appeal to the French government for relief from their intolerable conditions and asked Mendelssohn to draft an appropriate petition. Not wanting to undertake the task himself, he persuaded Christian Wilhelm von Dohm to undertake the defense of Alsatian Jewry. In response to Mendelssohn's request, von Dohm wrote the first systematic argument by a non-Jew in favor of Jewish emancipation, *Über die bürgerliche Verbesserung der Juden* ("Concerning the Civil Improvement of the Jews"), in 1781 and 1782. Dealing with the position of the Jews not only in Alsace but throughout Germany, von Dohm pointed out that they possessed all the necessary qualifications for citizenship. He recommended that Jews be granted specific civic rights

rather than the full rights of *citizenship*. They were not to hold public office or engage in political affairs, but they were to retain their own communal autonomy under government supervision, including the right to discipline recalcitrant members of the community and to maintain their own rabbinical courts.

Von Dohm's plea did not have immediate practical results, but it did place the question of Jewish rights in the center of public discussion. Numerous statements, some supporting von Dohm, others opposing and attacking his views, were published in the press. Mendelssohn realized that a centuries-old tradition of prejudice could not be silenced by a single courageous voice and that additional efforts were needed. He therefore induced another friend, the physician Markus Herz, to publish a German translation of *Vindiciae Judaeorum* by Manasseh ben Israel, whose defense of the Jews in 1656 had helped to persuade Oliver Cromwell to readmit Jews to England.

Mendelssohn himself wrote an extensive introduction to the translation. He wanted to add his voice to that of von Dohm and press home the attack against bigotry. But he also wanted to correct certain of von Dohm's views which, though well-intentioned, had been misconceived. His impression was that von Dohm himself was not wholly free from prejudice, as revealed, for example, in his view that Jews were not yet ready to receive the full rights of citizenship. Mendelssohn was also critical of von Dohm's proposal that the Jewish community should have the right to punish members for religious infractions or dissent. This proposal was incompatible with Mendelssohn's concept of religious freedom. For him, pure religion could not be coercive. Jews should be as free to believe and act as Christians were. In his passionate dissent, Mendelssohn put the responsibility where he felt it belonged: upon the prejudices and cruelty of the world [*Ed.*].

57. Manasseh ben Israel (1604?–1657), rabbi in Amsterdam, prolific author and negotiator on behalf of Jewish rights. Among his numerous works is *Vindiciae Judaeorum*, 1656, in which he refuted the objections of the British clergy, who wanted to debar the Jews from England. Mendelssohn wrote the introduction to the German translation of the work. See also note 47 [*Ed.*].

58. Herz Homberg (1749–1784), born in Lieben near Prague, was Mendelssohn's friend, his son's teacher, and collaborator on the commentary to Mendelssohn's translation of the Pentateuch. He later became superintendent of all Jewish schools in Galicia and resided in Prague [*Ed.*].

59. Sophie Becker, daughter and sister of clergymen; traveling companion of Elisa von der Recke, a member of the German aristocracy. Both were introduced to Mendelssohn by Nicolai in 1785 and remained in frequent correspondence with him [*Ed.*].

60. Mendelssohn gave several partially contradictory reasons for his decision to undertake a translation of the Pentateuch. In his Introduction to the translation as well as in a letter to Avigdor Levi (*GS*, XVI, 251), he stated that he had prepared the translation as a textbook for the private instruction of his sons. He consented to its publication only upon Solomon Dubno's insistence. Yet in his letter to Councilor Hennings he indicated that he had turned to this work because he had lost his capacity for quiet contemplation as a result of the Lavater incident. Moreover, he felt his efforts would benefit not only his children but his entire people. He conceived of the translation and commentary as a first step toward the acquisition of modern culture by the Jews of his time, something of which they stood in great need.

Not much later, he mentioned a third motive in a letter to Herder in which he disclosed that he had translated the Bible in order to provide his children with a resource that could serve as a spiritual armor against the inner and outer degradation to which they, like all Jews, were still subject. And in still another communication (a letter to Henoch), he expressed the hope that the new translation, though originally prepared mainly for the ordinary reader, would also have an impact on the rabbinical leaders of his time, who were in great need of more education and enlightenment.

The selections in this section illustrate this diversity of motivation [*Ed.*].

61. Elijah Bachur (1468–1549), generally known as Elijah Levita, was a noted grammarian and poet. He published a Judeo-German version of the Pentateuch, the Five Scrolls, and the Haf-

taroth, published in Constance, 1544. Isaac Jekutiel Blitz published a translation primarily for the use of Polish Jews who had fled to Amsterdam from the east. The work contained many Dutch expressions. The first edition of Rabbi Elijah's translation had actually been published in Venice. Mendelssohn's error is explained by his statement that he had never seen a copy of the book [*Ed.*].

62. August von Hennings first met Mendelssohn in Berlin, where he served as Councilor in the Danish embassy. He was helpful to Mendelssohn when his Bible translation was attacked in Jewish and non-Jewish circles [*Ed.*].

63. Johann Gottfried von Herder (1744–1803), German philosopher, poet, and critic. Herder was a pioneer in the fields of linguistics, comparative religion, and mythology and the author of numerous works, among them especially *Über den Ursprung der Sprache* and *Ideen zur Geschichte der Philosophie der Menscheit* [*Ed.*].

64. See note 24 [*Ed.*].

65. *Mishneh Torah*, Hilchot Teshuvah, VIII, 5 [*Ed.*].

66. Moses Nachmanides (Spain, 13th cent.), physician, mystic, Bible commentator [*Ed.*].

SOURCES

GENERAL SOURCES

SW   *Moses Mendelssohns sämmtliche Werke* (in one volume), Vienna, 1838.

GS   *Moses Mendelssohns gesammelte Schriften*, ed. by G. B. Mendelssohn, 7 vols., Leipzig, 1843–1844.

GSJA   *Moses Mendelssohn—Gesammelte Schriften*, Jubiläums Ausgabe (Jubilee edition), Berlin, 1930. Only seven volumes were completed.

INDIVIDUAL SOURCES

Jerusalem. SW, 217–291.

Letter to Johann Caspar Lavater. *GSJA*, VII, 7–17.

On Judaism and Christianity. From a letter to the Hereditary Prince of Braunschweig-Wolfenbüttel, *GSJA*, VII, 300–305.

On Revelation. From *Gegenbetrachtungen über Bonnets Palingenesie* (*Bonnet's Palingenesis: A Counterinquiry*), *GSJA*, VII, 65–107.

On Miracles. From a letter to Charles Bonnet, February 9, 1770, *GSJA*, VII, 321–325.

On Making Proselytes. From a letter to an unknown addressee, August 20, 1770, *GS*, V, 500; also in *Moses Mendelssohn: Zeugnisse, Briefe, Gespräche*, ed. by Bertha Badt-Strauss, Berlin, 1929, 190–191.

A Religion Without Dogma. 1. From a letter to Elkan Herz, July 23, 1771, *Moses Mendelssohn, sein Leben und Wirken*, by M. Kayserling, Leipzig, 1862 (1st edition), 495; 2. Badt-Strauss, *op. cit.*, 196–197; 3. from a letter to Wolf, July 11, 1782, *GS*, V, 601.

On the Immortality of the Soul. From *Phädon*, Second Dialogue, Part I, *SW*, 58.

On the Limitations of Religious Authority. From the Preface to a German translation of Manasseh ben Israel's *Vindiciae Judaeorum*, Berlin, March 19, 1782, *SW*, 694–695.

On Tolerance. 1. *Ibid.*, *SW*, 681–684, 697; 2. from a letter to Herz Homberg, March 1, 1784, *GS*, V, 669, 676.

On the Meaning of the Law. 1. From a letter to Herz Homberg, September 22, 1783, *GS*, V, 669, 676; 2. Badt-Strauss, *op. cit.*, 202–203; 3. from a letter to Sophie Becker, December 27, 1785, *GS*, V, 659.

A New Bible Translation. 1. From the Introduction to the translation of the Pentateuch, 1778, *GS*, VII, XVII ff.; see also *Moses Mendelssohn, eine Auswahl aus seinen Schriften und Briefen*, Frankfurt am Main, 1912, 55–57; 2. from a letter to Hennings, Strelitz, June 29, 1779, Kayserling, *op. cit.*, 531; 3. from a letter to Herder, Berlin, June 20, 1780, Kayserling, *op. cit.*, 543; 4. from a letter to Henoch, Berlin, March 30, 1780, Badt-Strauss, *op. cit.*, 221–222.

The Principles of Judaism: A Credo. From *Gegenbetrachtungen über Bonnets Palingenesie*, *GSJA*, VII, 95–99.

GUIDE FOR
FURTHER READING

MENDELSSOHN'S major Jewish writings were previously translated into English by M. Samuels and published under the title *Jerusalem*, 2 vols., London, 1838. Isaac Leeser published an English translation of *Jerusalem* as a "complement" to the periodical *The Occident*, Vol. IX, Philadelphia, 1852. However, both translations are antiquated and virtually inaccessible to the general reader.

The most detailed English account of Mendelssohn's life and work for the general reader can be found in Hermann Walter's *Moses Mendelssohn: Critic and Philosopher*, New York, 1930. Meyer Kayserling's *Moses Mendelssohn: Sein Leben und seine Werke*, Leipzig, 1862 (2nd edition, Leipzig, 1888), can be considered the most comprehensive of the numerous books on Mendelssohn that have appeared in the German language. The major facets of Mendelssohn's life and thought are also discussed in works such as *Moses Mendelssohn: Zur 200 jährigen Wiederkehr seines Geburtstages*, Berlin, 1929, which contains the essays "Moses Mendelssohn," by Bruno Strauss, "Die Philosophie Moses Mendelssohns," by Ernst Cassirer, "Moses Mendelssohns Wirken im Judentum," by Simon Bernfeld, and "Mendelssohn Literatur," by Hermann Meyer.

Accounts of Mendelssohn's life and work can also be found in H. Grätz, *History of the Jews*, Vol. V, Chap. 8; Shalom

Spiegel, *Hebrew Reborn*, Cleveland and New York, 1962, Chap. III; Alfred Jospe, "Moses Mendelssohn," in *Great Jewish Personalities in Modern Times*, ed. by Simon Noveck, Washington, D.C., 1960, 11–36; "Moses Mendelssohn: The Virtuous Jew" and "An Ephemeral Solution," by Michael A. Meyer, in *The Origins of the Modern Jew*, Detroit, 1967, 11–56; "Moses Mendelssohn: The German and Jewish Philosopher," by Simon Rawidowicz, in *Gaster Anniversary Volume*, London, 1936; "Moses Mendelssohn," by Simon Rawidowicz, *Hat'kufah*, XXII, 1929, 498–520 (Hebrew); and *Moses Mendelssohn: His Life and Times* by Maurice Simon, Jewish Religious Educational Publications, London, 1955.

The interested reader and student can turn to a number of scholarly monographs and articles for discussions of Mendelssohn's philosophical position, his concept of religion, and especially his views on Judaism. Jacob B. Agus summarizes Mendelssohn's thought in "The Age of Reason," *The Evolution of Jewish Thought*, New York, 1959, 371–395. Fritz Bamberger delineates "Mendelssohns Begriff vom Judentum," in *Korrespondenzblatt des Vereins zur Gründung und Erhaltung einer Akademie für die Wissenschaft des Judentums*, 1929, Vol. 10, 4–19 (reprinted in *Wissenschaft des Judentums im deutschen Sprachbereich: Ein Querschnitt*, II, Tübingen, 1967, 521–538). I. E. Barzilay examines Mendelssohn's ideas in "Moses Mendelssohn," *Jewish Quarterly Review*, LII, 1961, 69–93, 175–186. "Die Idee der Religion bei Lessing und Mendelssohn," by Ernst Cassirer, appears in *Festgabe zum zehnjährigen Bestehen der Akademie für die Wissenschaft des Judentums*, Berlin, 1929, 22–41. Yaakov Fleischmann examines Mendelssohn's views on Christianity in *Ba'ayat Ha'natzrut Bamachashavah Ha'yehudit mi-Mendelssohn ad Rosenzweig*, Jerusalem, 1964, 17–22. Julius Guttmann's chapter on Moses Mendelssohn in *Philosophies of Judaism*, New York, 1963, 291–303, presents a succinct over-all view of Mendelssohn's thought and his place in the history of Jewish and general philosophy. The same author explores similarities and differences in the systems of Mendelssohn and Spinoza in "Mendelssohns Jerusalem und Spinozas theologisch-politischer Traktat," in *Achtundvierzigster Bericht der Hochschule für die Wissenschaft des Judentums in Berlin,* 1931, 33–67. The question, To whom was Mendelssohn replying in *Jerusalem?* is discussed by Jacob Katz in a Hebrew article by that name in *Zion,* XXIX, 1–2, 1964, 112–132. Mendelssohn's views on the meaning of law in Jewish life are examined in Yitzhak Heinemann's *Ta'amei Hamitzvot b'Sifrut Yisrael,* II, Jerusalem, 1956, 9–47. David Patterson analyzes "Moses Mendelssohn's Concept of Tolerance," in *Between East and West,* ed. by A. Altmann, London, 1958, 149–163; Nathan Rothenstreich summarizes his research "On Mendelssohn's Political Philosophy" in *Yearbook XI of the Leo Baeck Institute,* London, 1966, 28–41. A critical analysis entitled "Mendelssohn's Character and Philosophy of Religion," by Walter Rothman, can be found in *CCAR Yearbook,* XXXIX, 1929, 305–350.

Alexander Altmann examines Mendelssohn's views on the question of Spinoza's possible influence on Leibnitz in "Moses Mendelssohn on Leibnitz and Spinoza," in *Studies in Rationalism, Judaism and Universalism,* ed. by R. Loewe, London, 1966, 13–45. I. E. Barzilay traces the background of the Berlin *Haskalah* in *Essays on Jewish Life and Thought Presented in Honor of Salo Wittmayer Baron,* New York, 1959, 183–197. Mendelssohn's influence on the *Haskalah* in Eastern Europe is summarized by J. Klausner, *Historia shel Ha'sifrut Ha'ivrit Ha'hadashah,* Jerusalem, 1930–1950, I, 33–87.

Finally, virtually complete bibliographies covering Mendelssohn's own writings as well as writings on Mendelssohn can be found in Hermann Meyer's "Mendelssohn Literatur," in *op. cit.,* 99–138, and especially in Michael A. Meyer, *op. cit.,* 221–227.